Living With
EEYORE

Living With EEYORE

HOW TO POSITIVELY LOVE
THE NEGATIVE PEOPLE IN YOUR LIFE

ELIZABETH BAKER

Standard®
PUBLISHING
Bringing The Word to Life
Cincinnati, Ohio

Published by Standard Publishing, Cincinnati, Ohio
www.standardpub.com

Published in association with the literary agency of WordServe Literary Group, Ltd., 10152 S. Knoll Circle, Highlands Ranch, Colorado 80130.

Printed in the United States of America

Project editor: Lynn Lusby Pratt
Cover and interior design: DogEared Design
Author photo: Treasured Moments Photography

All Scripture quotations, unless otherwise indicated, are taken from the *New King James Version* of the Bible. Copyright © 1982 by Thomas Nelson, Inc. Used by permission. All rights reserved. Scriptures marked *NIV* are taken from THE HOLY BIBLE, NEW INTERNATIONAL VERSION®. NIV®. Copyright © 1973, 1978, 1984 by International Bible Society. Used by permission of Zondervan. All rights reserved.

The epigraphs that begin each chapter are taken from *The Complete Tales & Poems of Winnie-the-Pooh* by A. A. Milne (New York: Dutton's Children's Books, 2001).

ISBN 0-7847-1962-4

Library of Congress Cataloging-in-Publication Data
Baker, Elizabeth, 1944-
    Living with Eeyore : how to positively love the negative people in your life / Elizabeth Baker.
    p. cm.
    ISBN 0-7847-1962-4
    1. Interpersonal conflict--Religious aspects--Christianity. 2. Spiritual formation. 3. Interpersonal relations--Religious aspects--Christianity. 4. Love--Religious aspects--Christianity. 5. Negativism. 6. Eeyore (Fictitious character) I. Title.

BV4597.53.C58B35 2007
248.4--dc22   2006014869
   13 12 11 10 09 08 07   9 8 7 6 5 4 3 2 1

For my own favorite Eeyore,
whose giftedness has benefited
my life in every way.

CONTENTS

— · · · · · —

CHAPTER ONE

An Eeyore of Your Very Own

"Good morning, Pooh Bear," said Eeyore gloomily. "If it is a good morning," he said. "Which I doubt."

· · · · · · · · ·

"I shouldn't be surprised if it hailed a good deal tomorrow," Eeyore was saying. "Blizzards and what-not. Being fine today doesn't Mean Anything."

have come to the conclusion that somewhere in our lives we all need at least one Eeyore. This must be true, or God would not have made so many of them. With a sigh, a little cloud, and amazing regularity, Eeyores settle into our Hundred Acre Wood, and suddenly life is not as simple as it was before.

Kathy's* mom seems always to have been an Eeyore. At least, she has been since Kathy was a child. Unfortunately, Mom is becoming more Eeyoreish with age. Most of the time, Kathy manages to respond to her mother's stream of negative comments in a kind, rational manner, but on the worst days the negativism overwhelms her best intentions.

It was Saturday, and Kathy was driving her mother to the store. The trip had started out well enough, and then Kathy shared news about her daughter, Valerie, who had won a position on the dance team. Mom countered that she hoped it didn't make her vain or cause her to be morally tempted. "That happens to so many girls these days," she said.

Kathy changed the subject and remarked that the weather was unusually dry for the time of year. Mom agreed but quickly went into a discussion of a report she had heard on TV. The world would soon be coming to an end because of the

---

*Case stories in this book are compilations based on real people, but details and all names have been changed.

9

greenhouse effect. All the scientists said so, and the dry weather proved it was true.

Kathy switched to the topic of groceries. There was a sale on tomatoes at Tom Thumb. Mom didn't like tomatoes and was sure that everything she had on her list would be much higher this week.

Peppered in between these comments, Kathy heard about the fact that she was driving too fast, that her boss was making her work too much, and that she was looking pale.

Kathy gave up. A brief silence followed, and then Mom started talking about her little dog. She needed to prepare herself to lose Trixie. No, the dog was not sick. It was just that dogs did not live very long, and if Trixie got sick, Mom could not afford the vet bills.

Kathy didn't know whether to scream or to pound her head against the steering wheel. It was going to be a looooong shopping trip!

Shopping is always difficult when you have Eeyore in tow.

You do remember Eeyore, don't you? That gloomy, gray donkey made famous by Winnie the Pooh? Eeyore was consistently negative, always sad, and never admitted that the glass was really half full. Eeyore knew the glass would always be half empty and probably had a leak in the bottom as well. I assume you have an Eeyore somewhere in your life. Most everyone does.

(Note: In order to avoid a ridiculous repetition of he/ she or slavishly adhere to using a male pronoun one time and female the next, most of the references to Eeyore in this book will be male. My apologies to men who are in relationship with female Eeyores, but I am sure you can relate nonetheless.)

Eeyores come in both sexes and all ages. God has sprinkled them liberally in churches, families, and businesses. Some are severe types with medication in hand, and some are little gray clouds that sigh a lot. What makes them all Eeyores is the fact that they consistently see the negative, point out what others are doing wrong, drag their heels when new ideas are suggested, and generally complicate relationships.

Living peacefully with Eeyore and learning to love him is not an easy task. Your Eeyore may be a moody teenage son who is sure he will never succeed at anything. Or maybe she is a mother-in-law who continually apologizes for taking up space on planet Earth. The Eeyore whom God has put in your path may be a mate who forecasts doom and gloom when you want to buy a new car. Or he may be a boss who is continually finding the dark side of every possibility. One thing is for sure: you either have an Eeyore in your life, or you are playing the role of Eeyore in someone else's life!

Stuffed animals can be pricey, especially if they are well-made, genuine copies of the original. But human Eeyores are available for free, and you don't even have to seek them out. If you don't currently have one, just be patient and one is sure to find you. Eeyores are so prevalent, it is even possible to have more than one! Their plenitude suggests they are a needed element in God's ecology and proof that the Almighty has a sense of humor.

The original Eeyore lived in a quiet corner of the Hundred Acre Wood in the Thistle Patch that he seldom left. He sighed a lot. Much of Pooh Bear's energy went into trying to understand and cheer this fellow creature who was so very different from himself. Pooh had a positive outlook; and although he occasionally complained, "Oh, bother," he trusted that tomorrow would bring sunshine. He was basically content with life and satisfied with simple, pleasant thoughts. Eeyore was not.

Like Pooh, you may have spent a fair amount of time scratching your head and trying to figure out this fellow creature. Puzzling about how to communicate with, fix, cheer, and understand Eeyore can be quite a task. That task is made considerably more difficult in a real world where opposites often attract. This strange attraction has created some very interesting marriages. It has also caused some very unhappy endings. But most of all, it has fostered situations in which two people look at each other in rapt curiosity, wondering how in the world the other could possibly be thinking, feeling, or doing that particular thing.

I have known quite a few Eeyores in my time. Some were clients who came to my counseling office for help with depression. Those were the easiest Eeyores for me to deal with. At other times Eeyore was someone I had to go to church with, work for, or live with. Not so easy.

When I treat an Eeyore for depression, the battlefield is outside myself. My concern and activity take place in a world where I am only an interested observer and coach. But when I work alongside or live with Eeyore, the battle comes home. My personal world gets frustrated, convoluted, and painful. I must deal with my own communication style, character growth, and eternal reward. Ugh. It is much easier to sit across the room and give advice than it is to take some biblical concepts home and make them work.

Yet I must admit that life would be far more dull without Eeyore. He may not be the life of the party, but Eeyore can be a reason the party is given. Eeyore presents an opportunity to stretch beyond ourselves. He can provide the balance we need and often is a source of good advice. His attitude may primarily be shades of gray, but that very somber tone can make the colors of life more vivid and welcome.

There is a use for everything in God's economy. He never wastes a detail or sends useless things to his children. Why, even manure is beneficial when applied in the right amounts to the proper places! It is only reasonable that everything in our lives has a benevolent purpose—even when God sends an Eeyore to be your very own.

> GET THE POINT

There is a use for everything in God's economy, even difficult people.

> > READ THE BOOK

Read Romans 8:28, 29.

1. Who can be assured of the promise that God will work all things for their good?

2. What primary goal is God working toward in our lives (v. 29)?

Check out Isaiah 45:6, 7.

1. What type of things do these Scripture verses indicate are controlled by God?

(Note: If using the *KJV,* be aware that "evil" does not always involve a moral connotation but can refer to anything worth rejection or useless for the intended purpose. Refer also to Jeremiah 24:1-3 in the *KJV.)*

Read Job 1:6–2:13; 42:1-6, 10-13.

1. Satan had to ask God's permission before he could attack Job. How does that make you feel?

2. How did the trials that came to Job change his view of God?

Read Luke 12:6, 7.

1. How many things about your life are unknown to God?

2. How should that make you respond to negative people with whom you have a relationship?

> > > TELL THE TRUTH

1. Recall a time when you learned and grew spiritually because of the presence of a difficult person in your life.

2. Have you ever doubted that God could make good things come out of a situation you found personally painful?

3. Are you currently in relationship with someone you believe possesses a personality similar to Eeyore's?

—•••••—

CHAPTER TWO

Eeyore's Problem

The old grey donkey, Eeyore, stood by himself in a thistly corner of the forest . . . and thought about things. Sometimes he thought sadly to himself, "Why?" and sometimes he thought, "Wherefore?" and sometimes he thought, "Inasmuch as which?"—and sometimes he didn't quite know what he was thinking about.

•••••••••

Eeyore . . . stood by the side of the stream, and looked at himself in the water.

"Pathetic," he said. "That's what it is. Pathetic."

When God puts an Eeyore in your path, the first thing any just-get-up-and-do-it, stick-a-flower-in-your-hair-and-be-happy type of person assumes is that something must be wrong with this morose creature who spends so much time in sad contemplation. Surely he's sick, broken, unspiritual, or at least suffering from a low self-image. But if you are going to build a successful bridge to Eeyore and stay very long in relationship with him, one of the first things you need to know is that he probably is not sick and doesn't necessarily need to be fixed.

It may come as a shock to a generation brought up on TV commercials and political hype, but negative feelings are a normal part of human existence. Expect them. Not only is it normal for all of us to be negative part of the time, there are certain personalities who make a career out of noticing the downside of every up and the cloud in every sunny day. This does not mean they are sick and does not always indicate a need for medication. But on the other hand, it may.

This brings us to an interesting quandary. How do we know when Eeyore is sick and when he is just being his usual cloudy self? Those living with an Eeyore are sometimes deeply perplexed—wondering whether they should call the doctor or just smack Eeyore one and tell him to get over it!

It isn't easy to give a clear answer to the question. However, there are some guidelines to help steer you through the fog. These are the same guidelines used by professionals. Learning a little about them might save Eeyore a knot on the noggin!

Is Eeyore Sick?

Professionals have tried to codify the difference between mentally sick and emotionally healthy for almost a hundred years. Frankly, the job they have done has been fair to middlin' at best, but at least they have tried. Their current offering is the *Diagnostic and Statistical Manual IV-TR*, or *DSM* for short. Basically, it is a list of observed behaviors and subjectively reported feelings that have been arranged in similar groupings and then given a title and number. For example, if you are otherwise healthy but can't remember who you are—and it is apparent that this circumstance happened suddenly—then you probably have disease 294.8, amnesic disorder not otherwise specified.

Since the *DSM* was first published, it has gone through at least a dozen changes.[1] What at one time was a disease becomes normal with the next edition, and vice versa. Complicating things still further, various countries have their own versions of the *DSM*. It is possible to have a recognized mental disease in America while the same behavior is considered normal in Europe!

As of the moment, the criteria for diagnosing major depression involve nine characteristics:[2]

1. A depressed mood most of the day, nearly every day
2. Markedly diminished pleasure in daily activity
3. Significant weight loss
4. Insomnia or hypersomnia nearly every day
5. Psychomotor agitation or retardation
6. Fatigue
7. Feelings of worthlessness
8. Diminished ability to think or concentrate
9. Recurrent thoughts of death

Officially, to be depressed you need only a two-week period in which you can say yes to five of the nine items. In other words, it is not too difficult to officially have the mental disease of major depressive disorder. Many folks go through it at least once in their lives. Some stay there for decades.

Is your Eeyore sick? Maybe. Eeyore-type people are more prone to experiencing depression that is severe enough to diagnose, and they get depressed more often than their more positive peers. Medications bring some relief to most people, and in some cases meds can be lifesaving. It is not a sign of spiritual weakness to take medications, and in some rare cases people productively stay on them for years. But since most depression naturally abates within a few weeks, don't be too quick to assume Eeyore's solution is in a medicine bottle. Maybe Eeyore is sick . . . but maybe not.

If you are worried about your Eeyore, look over the criteria for major depression and ask a few questions. If the behavior you are seeing is significantly different from what you have seen in the past, and if week after week goes by without an improvement, encourage Eeyore to visit a counselor or your family physician. Only the most severe forms of depression need the help of a psychiatrist.

The amazing truth is, there's a good chance nothing is wrong with your Eeyore. He doesn't need fixing. She is probably not broken. Eeyores are just different from other personality types. *Much* different. If you have determined that your Eeyore probably is not sick, understanding those differences and accepting them can go a long way toward creating peace.

Knowing a little more about what the world looks like when viewed through Eeyore's eyes is one way to help you live in peace while you're simultaneously building dikes that will keep you from drowning in his sea of negativity! But understanding Eeyore is not always easy. Here are some places to look for clues.

Family Background, Transference, and Unresolved Emotions

Eeyore did not drop in from another planet. He comes from Adam's stock, and the same dynamics that shape him influence us all. Three of these dynamics are family background, psychological defense mechanisms such as transference, and the complicated reality of repressed emotions that sprout years later as problem behaviors. These common forces should not be considered illnesses. Eeyore is not sick when he experiences these; he is simply struggling through a few of the realities of life in a fallen world. All of us will be impacted by family background, defense mechanisms like transference, and unresolved emotions—and all of us need to understand and grow past them.

Read over the following examples and comments and see if one or more of them might apply to your Eeyore. Give thought and prayer to any that seem to fit. The understanding you gain will not change a thing as far as Eeyore's negative approach to life is concerned, but it may change your emotional reaction to his negativity. When all is said and done, that is the main goal we are after. Your peace comes first. Changing Eeyore is second.

Family Background

Every person has been significantly shaped by his family of origin. The past is inescapable. Eeyore grew up in an environment too. Understanding that environment will be invaluable for helping to provide peace.

An age span of almost twenty years separated Janice from her husband, Fred. Her past was sinful; his was pure. She became a Christian in her forties and at the time of their marriage was a new believer. Fred had known the Scriptures since childhood and had served many years as a deacon in the church. Janice had been divorced twice. He had been widowed once. She was a friend of his daughter. Their May-December romance was a dream come true for both of them.

Janice was a product of the rebellious '60s. Fred was born at the end of the Great Depression and lived through WWII as a young boy. It did not take long for the baggage of the past and personal idiosyncrasies to catch up with this happy couple. It was not that they fell out of love or fought all the time; it was just that his negative don't-risk-it, don't-spend-it lifestyle and her entrepreneurial let's-go-for-broke spirit clashed to the point that it made them both dizzy.

To some extent, they would always be from different worlds. But for Janice, the gulf between them became a bit more tolerable when she read a novel about the Great Depression. She had, of course, known about those years from her history books, but for the first time she began to emotionally connect with the feeling of desperation experienced by many during that time. Her understanding expanded even more when she spent a slow, summer afternoon listening to Fred talk about what it was like growing up.

Fred's youth had included true hunger and continual fear of an uncertain future. It was no wonder that he was cautious and wanted to save every penny possible. Janice thought how this contrasted with her own life. There had never been a single

24

thing she wanted that she couldn't eventually afford or a single goal that she had not achieved.

This insight did not eliminate all the stress Janice felt in the relationship. It did not change Fred's tendency to be overly cautious and negative. However, it did help her put his I-told-you-it-would-never-work-out attitude in perspective. She learned to take his warnings of "don't spend it," "don't risk it," and "don't do it" less personally and found it less irksome to yield when he worried too much about a decision she wanted to make.

Think about your Eeyore's background. Did he frequently have to change schools and peer groups? Was there any alcohol or drug abuse that made life uncertain from day to day? Did she have to take on the responsibility of sheltering small siblings when she was only ten? Did he lose his dad and have to become the man of the house while still a preteen? If so, these may be part of the reason Eeyore is skittish, always expects the worst, or is afraid to take risks.

Perhaps your Eeyore constantly criticizes everyone and always sees situations in the worst possible light. Have you looked at his family? Maybe he grew up under a constant barrage of criticism. Did his parents pick apart everyone they knew and look for the tiniest flaw in every situation? It would be hard for a child to grow up under that burden and not become critical.

Being aware of Eeyore's past may increase your ability

to put his negativity in perspective. Understanding that you too have realities from your past that influence how you react today may give you additional courage and grace when Eeyore's comments start to grate on your nerves. We all are works in progress and can afford to be forgiving.

Transference

Another dynamic that shapes our behavior is the phenomenon of transference. *Transference* is a Freudian term that is far too complicated to discuss adequately in this book. But we can learn some things about the concept that can help us relate peacefully to Eeyore.

The best way to understand transference is by seeing it in action. If an employee is mad at his boss but must smile in order to keep his job, and if he comes home and kicks the dog, that is transference. Transference occurs when we take emotions that should go one place, but because it is not safe to express them in that direction, we transfer them to a target that is likely to cause us less trouble. If the Eeyore in your life seems to be OK around everyone but you, look for transference.

John had never learned to relate well to women, but he and Susan married after a fairly uneventful courtship and settled into a cordial, if distant, relationship. The situation remained stable until John's father died, and at the couple's invitation, John's mother moved in next door.

John's mother always needed something. The roof had a leak. She did not understand a doctor's bill. She was out of milk. The cat needed to go to the vet. Making matters worse, she was close enough to become John's mommy again. He ought to eat better. He shouldn't cut the lawn so short in hot weather. He should spend more time with her. He ought to ask his boss for a raise.

John was always patient with his mom, but he became increasingly critical of Susan. John was fine at work, at peace in the presence of his mother, cooperative and cheerful at church or with friends. But in the privacy of home, he was gloomy, critical, and angry. Nearly every statement directed at Susan was about what was wrong with her and the house and the children. It got so bad, she felt as though her very breathing irritated him.

When the change first began to take place in John, Susan was angry. His silence had been bad enough, but this new attitude was unbearable. How dare he become so critical and negative! She had done nothing wrong!

Slowly, the truth of the situation began to come to light. Susan really had done nothing wrong. She could not possibly be the cause of the change in John. When she considered the timing of the change, it seemed far more likely to be something about John's mom. John was upset with his mom for getting older and needing his help—and upset with himself for being upset! Susan realized that she wasn't the problem but had become the target.

Wisely, she did not confront John directly. Instead, Susan prayed and received grace to take his criticisms lightly and even with a bit of humor. She refused to play the role of wounded martyr. At the same time, she carefully offered invitations for John to talk about his feelings. And when things became very tense, she gently but firmly told him his attitude was sinful—and calmly walked away.

Knowing that she was not the real target of John's negativity did not solve Susan's problem, but it did ease the pain. It also gave her a plan of action.

The good news is that within a few months, John himself realized the source of his problem. He repented and learned to serve his mom with both compassionate care and the proper boundaries that allowed him to breathe.

If the Eeyore in your life appears to show his negative side only in relationship with you, and if after honest soul-searching you can think of no reason why this should be, you would be justified in assuming that some kind of transference might be the culprit.

Susan was fortunate in that she figured out fairly quickly what was going on, and her assessment of the situation was accurate. But not all situations are so easily understood. It is good to think about possible antecedents for Eeyore's attitudes, but don't spend excessive effort trying to unravel Eeyore's subconscious mind. In most cases, Eeyore himself will have no idea why you "bring out the worst" in him.

If the reason why is not obvious, be content to know that the problem was not created by anything you did . . . and respond accordingly.

Knowing you are a target of transference will not fix things, but it can take away some of the pressure. You may offer subtle opportunities for Eeyore to talk about issues, but resist the temptation to show him what is *really* going on. In the first place, you may be wrong. In the second place, even if you are right, nothing will change unless the Lord reveals the problem to Eeyore. Just accept the fact that even though you are the target of the negativism, you are probably not the true villain at which Eeyore is aiming!

Unresolved Emotions

Our ability to experience emotion is one of the ways in which we are created in God's image. Deuteronomy 29:23 and Psalm 95:10 describe God's anger. But in our frail human state, we don't always know what to do with feelings such as anger or grief. When mismanaged, our effort to control such powerful emotions can create more problems than it solves.

The correct way to manage strong and potentially destructive emotions is with the two-pronged spear of truth and humility.

Truth. We must fully embrace the emotion, own the full limit of the struggle, and face the raging feelings head-on without a sugarcoating of denial.

Humility. We must completely release control, letting God be the final judge and sovereign authority in our lives. We must forgive and accept forgiveness. But achieving the right balance between embracing and releasing is far from easy.

When we mismanage powerful emotions and fail to either completely embrace the pain or release control, the emotions can bury themselves like the root of a noxious weed that sprouts again when most unexpected to spoil the landscape of our lives. Julia discovered this truth when the seeds sown in her teens bore fruit as she neared forty.

Under any circumstance Julia would have been considered a plain girl. But when her quiet personality, drab hair, and large nose were added to the ungraceful limbs and overgrown body of junior high age, she was almost ugly. Besides all this, her sister, Sarah, was charming, petite, and the darling of her father's attention. In every way Sarah outshined, outperformed, and surpassed Julia on every point by which the world measures success.

As the years passed, Julia outgrew some of her homeliness. She learned how to dress and how to walk without tripping over her own feet. But these accomplishments paled when compared to the grace and charm of her older sister. And no matter how much she improved, her father made no secret of the fact that Sarah was his favorite and always would be.

Eventually, the sisters married and, from all outward appearances, led remarkably similar lives. There was no obvious resentment between them. Grandchildren came along. Time passed. Mom and Dad grew old.

Throughout most of her life, Julia had been a classic Eeyore. But after thirteen years of marriage, her times of being "down" and crying "for no reason" became more frequent and severe— as did the unexpected fear that occasionally gripped her.

Did Julia need medication? Maybe. But Julia's main problem was not her brain chemistry as much as it was her grief and anger over childhood issues that she had long ago buried rather than resolved.

One day in a counselor's office, Julia lost it and was shocked that the pain, anger, and shame came pouring out in a torrent. At first Julia was frightened by the intense emotions, but over time she would learn what it meant to resolve them within a Christian context.

The past would always hurt a bit, and all her life she would probably have times when she had to stand against the temptation of jealousy. But when she finished working on these issues with honesty and humility, the past no longer controlled her. She learned to deal with—rather than hide from—strong feelings, and her Eeyore tendencies were no longer exacerbated by unresolved emotions.

Julia was in her late thirties by the time she sought counseling. Sarah, at forty, still commanded most of their father's attention and love. Sarah was still a beauty, and Julia was not. Sarah had a perky and positive outlook on life. To Julia, the cup would always be half empty. But Julia also had a *new degree of peace. She understood herself better and accepted her lot in life with more grace. Even though her sad history was unchanged, when she finally admitted the pain and fully embraced it, she experienced offering and receiving forgiveness at a deeply emotional level. Later, she learned how she could put her hurt within the context of a sovereign God and eternity. That brought peace.*

Your Eeyore, like Julia, may have one or more painful realities in the past that contribute to a gloomy outlook on life and the expectation of disaster. If so, counseling, spiritual growth, or a safe place to talk over the past with a trusted friend can release some of the pressure and help Eeyore achieve a better balance in life.

But then again . . . maybe not.

Just Being Eeyore

As stated at the beginning of this chapter, your Eeyore may need medical attention. Depression is certainly a sickness, and it can be treated. However, just because someone habitually sees the glass as half empty, prefers to spend time alone, and has a gloomy outlook on life does not necessarily mean he is sick.

Your Eeyore may be a dyed-in-the-wool, 110-percent-gloom-city kind of pessimist, or he may be of the on-again-off-again, more-or-less, mostly-see-the-dark-side variety.

But every Eeyore has similar basic tendencies; that is what makes them Eeyores.

The primary characteristic of all Eeyores is that they are problem vigilant. They also avoid responsibility, withdraw, and are given to excessive thinking. But the most burdensome of all their tendencies is the continual stream of negative comments and conclusions that are applied to every situation and each conversation. Every Eeyore may not show all of these tendencies all of the time, but these behaviors will be very familiar to anyone who has been very long in relationship with an Eeyore.

Problem Vigilant

It is ingrained in the very nature of Eeyores to focus on problems. Big problems. Little problems. Today's problems. Tomorrow's problems. Hypothetical problems. And problems that might develop someday if the situation is just right.

A mother Eeyore notices every frivolous dollar that her adult child spends, each grandchild's thank-you note that was sent too late, the dust in the corner of the living room that should have been removed last week, and whether little Alex is growing as fast as his father grew.

When Eeyore is a boss, he micromanages. Every detail is scrutinized, and chances are that whatever you did, wrote, or said was wrong. There will seldom be any acknowledgment of special circumstances, your skill level, or a past history of success.

Eeyores are often mentally sharp—an old donkey has a memory like an elephant. This makes the problem search even more expansive as every detail from the past comes to the forefront. A teenage Eeyore can remember every little thing his parents did wrong from the time he was three. A wife Eeyore keeps a mental scoreboard on her husband that goes back decades.

Responsibility Avoidant

Eeyores are masters at pointing out problems but lousy at solving them! They seem to expect others to fix the problems while they sit back and point out holes in proposed solutions.

Eeyores are not necessarily lazy, but actually fixing things doesn't seem to be on their mental screens. Eeyores may do their jobs well and put a lot of energy into projects they have chosen, but they seldom voluntarily choose—and more often wait for others—to fix things. They analyze, pick apart, and criticize but are rarely willing to take responsibility for resolution!

Withdrawal

Eeyores have a tendency to withdraw from others and isolate themselves. Often this is a physical withdrawal, but it can be an emotional withdrawal that leaves others feeling isolated even when they are so close they could reach out and touch. One of the loneliest places on earth may be the room where you are sitting with an Eeyore you love but can't emotionally reach. Eeyores seem to have a special ability to pull inside themselves and study the world outside their skins without actually partaking of it. Others can feel the separation even if they can't put it in words.

Excessive Thinking

No one can think something to death quite like Eeyores. They turn each situation, idea, or person over and over in their minds, examining them for every flaw and danger. When they're talking out loud, you will often hear them repeat the same sentences as they reason in circles around the same topic. Each time a positive aspect of the object under scrutiny is found, they can't let go until they can find a corresponding negative aspect. The whys and wherefores go on forever, echoing in a bottomless well.

Negative Comments and Conclusions

Eeyore is drawn to problems like bees are drawn to honey. The two are inseparable. This irresistible focus on problems is one reason why most everything out of Eeyore's mouth sounds negative. Shopping? The blouse costs too much, the color is wrong, and the fabric will probably come apart. Driving? The lights are changing too slowly, the other driver made a stupid move, and the exhaust from cars is making his allergies worse. Sitting in church? The preacher was good but could improve if he would study more, the auditorium was too hot, and the choir sang that same hymn last month.

It has been my experience with Eeyores that they often do not hear their observations as negative or complaining. To them, it is just normal conversation. But to those listening who are of a more positive outlook, the words can feel like a heavy burden. It is like the sun being repeatedly eclipsed.

Just because Eeyore is not sick doesn't mean he doesn't have problems that need the healing of the Savior and the help of a friend. He may not be wrong or broken or suffering from diagnosable disease, but just like any other human, he has habits and reactions that need changing. We can help him change for the better, and being in relationship with him can help us change too.

Eeyores may not need fixing, but when we Tiggers and Piglets and Rabbits have to live with them, we may need a special set of skills in order to survive! Skills that help us talk to Eeyore in a way that helps him understand. Skills that let us listen to him without being overwhelmed by the negative flood. We also need skills of self-protection, for we may not be comfortable in Eeyore's Thistle Patch; we may need to learn how to preserve our corner of the Hundred Acre Wood and decorate the space with a little more sunshine.

Yet there is another skill that is even more important than talking, listening, and protecting our sunshine. Using this skill, we can learn to view Eeyore as a friend, not an enemy. He may be different from us. At times he may irritate, frustrate, and challenge us to the max. But Eeyore is not our enemy, and the first step toward seeing him in the light of friendship is to identify the gifts God has given him and to rejoice in how those gifts benefit our lives.

Sound impossible? It is. Because, in truth, continually walking with positive appreciation for others is more than just a skill that determined people learn. It is a grace from the Spirit.

> GET THE POINT

Even though someone may irritate you, he or she is not necessarily sick, weird, or flawed.

> > READ THE BOOK

Examine 1 Samuel 16:14-23; 18:5-16; 31:3-6.

1. The full story of King Saul covers most of the book of 1 Samuel. The above references give some highlights of his life. After reading these sections, would you diagnose Saul with clinical depression? Why or why not?

2. What, if anything, made Saul feel better?

Read 1 Kings 19:1-18.

1. Elijah had just returned from a solid victory over the prophets of Baal at Mount Carmel, when things suddenly changed. Read the story and decide whether you believe Elijah was depressed.

2. What steps did the angel take to help Elijah feel better? How do you think these steps would help depression?

3. What steps did God take? How do you think these steps would help depression?

Check out Acts 17:5-10.

1. Transference is the shifting of strong emotion from the real target to a safer, more convenient one. Who were the real targets in this story?

2. If you had been Jason, what would have been your response? What would be the ideal response?

> > > TELL THE TRUTH

1. What is your opinion about using medication to help with problem moods?

2. How has your family background guided your response to certain situations?

3. The author described Eeyore as being problem vigilant, responsibility avoidant, withdrawn, given to excessive thinking, and communicating in a negative manner. How many of these characteristics describe the Eeyore in your life?

4. Embracing an emotion (truth) and then releasing it to the care of God's sovereignty (humility) are said to provide resolution for painful emotions. Have you ever experienced this process? What was the outcome?

CHAPTER THREE

———• • • • • •———

Eeyore's Gifts

"It's snowing still," said Eeyore gloomily.

"So it is."

"And freezing."

"Is it?"

"Yes," said Eeyore. "However," he said, brightening up a little, "we haven't had an earthquake lately."

I once thought that God and Eeyore were enemies. It was as though God were trying his best to reach me with a smattering of blessings, but Eeyore stood obstinately in the way, blocking the process. The Almighty would pitch a morsel of peace in my direction, and Eeyore would swing his bat, knocking it back to the sky. God would design a stream of encouragement and send it rolling like a river. Eeyore would dig an even deeper trench in my life and rechannel the flow. Surprisingly, time has proved me totally wrong.

Eeyore is not blocking God. He is facilitating everything the Almighty desires and is giving wonderful gifts to everyone with whom he comes in contact. These gifts may look a little strange because they often come wrapped in the paper of frustration, but they are real gifts just the same. Years of being bumped, prodded, and blocked by various Eeyores have given me abundant proof of this, and I suspect—if you are willing to look past the wrapping—you will find that your Eeyore offers gifts to you too. Learning to be grateful for those gifts can go a long way toward offering hope and smoothing the rough spots in a relationship.

Like all good gifts, the presents that Eeyore provides ultimately find their source in the hand of God (James 1:17, 18). God is not helplessly blocked and struggling to get around Eeyore. The Almighty blesses what Eeyore naturally offers and uses it to create good. These gifts don't come to us fighting their way around the obstacle of Eeyore's negative nature. They exist precisely because of it.

Eeyore doesn't have to change a thing in order to shower you with good gifts. It doesn't matter if your Eeyore is simply a mildly negative personality or a perpetual reservoir of gloom and doom. There will be ways that Eeyore enhances your life, builds your character, and adds richness to your eternal reward. All without a single smile.

The Gift of Balance

Joel and Kathleen Lockney had been married for thirty-five years. Kathleen was a classic Eeyore and knew it. Joel considered himself rational, adult, and balanced in every way.

Their years together had been basically happy. Three children had come, and three children had gone. Two were now married, and one was in the last year of college. Jobs and careers had come, and many of those jobs and careers left with the couple's blessing. Joel had worked at four jobs before landing his current career as an electrician with the local power plant. Kathleen's on-again, off-again work outside the home had taken several forms. Her most recent excursion into the business world had ended six months ago when Tracy's Dresses closed and no longer needed a part-time bookkeeper.

Through the years the Lockneys' relationship followed the normal peaks and valleys that were expected. Joel and Kathleen irritated each other and adjusted to each other through a thousand and one situations. He stood his ground; she gave in. She stood her ground; he gave in. As the Bible warned would happen, iron had sharpened iron (Proverbs 27:17), and they were both better for the sparks.

If you had pulled each aside for a private cup of coffee and asked about their years together, both would have said the years were good. And both would have candidly claimed that they had given in to their mate far more often than the reverse had been true. Only God knew the actual score.

But the amiable years and generous give-and-take were forgotten one cold night, February 10. They sat on opposite sides of the kitchen table. Their future was on the line, and nothing would be the same again. Kathleen was frightened and in tears. Joel was sullen and stubbornly resistant. He was not about to give in to her gloomy predictions.

The first rumblings of this fight had sounded before Christmas when a friend from Joel's work retired. He was two years younger than Joel. The more Joel thought on it, the more he envied his friend's freedom. When the company offered an incentive bonus for any employee willing to leave the company payroll for a rocking chair, Joel wanted to jump at the chance. The bonus would almost buy a used motor home. Throw in some savings and a couple of garage sales, and he and Kathleen could spend the rest of their years on the road fishing, making new friends, and dropping in unexpectedly to hug the grandkids.

Kathleen panicked. At first, her arguments were emotional outbursts that mixed the sure fall of the U.S. economic system with how Joel never could be depended on to think through a situation. But as the days of January faded and the company deadline for a final decision grew nearer, her bookkeeper mind kicked into gear. She pulled mortality charts from the Internet, worked graphs predicting income and expenses, and completed a spreadsheet with black numbers that faded into red. The company deadline was February 15. On the evening of the tenth, she presented her charts and fears to Joel. The verdict was clear: they would be broke at least nine years before they were likely to be dead.

Joel was angry. Like always, Kathleen had picked out the worst-case scenario and followed every negative detail she could find. How could anyone know that gas prices would rise during the next ten years at the same rate they had the last ten? She had not even considered the fact that he would be picking up odd jobs along the way. He did not like her charts and figures. And at the moment, he did not like his wife much either!

Joel brooded and reminded Kathleen of how she spent her life being negative. He pulled up the past and pounded her with every predicted tragedy that had not come true and every fear that was never realized. He knew her weak spots and that she would eventually give in if he expressed enough anger and forced her to doubt herself. His pride, weariness with the day-to-day grind of work, and desire for the good life drove him to ignore her warnings.

Joel would get his way. Pity. The couple would have been so much better off had he remembered that Eeyore brings gifts as well as difficulties to any relationship. Joel's unrealistic, rosy view of the future needed to be balanced. He was blowing right past the caution light that the Holy Spirit had put in his path.

One of the most beneficial things about relationship with an Eeyore is also one of the most irritating: the uncanny way he can find the single flaw in everything from fresh produce to political speeches. Murphy's Law may tell you a thing is more likely to fail than to succeed, but it takes an Eeyore to tell you exactly what the fatal flaw will be and to predict the earliest date of collapse. There is no one who can pop a dream bubble quite like Eeyore.

Like any child of Adam, we all want *what* we want, *when* we want it. But those of us who thrive on silver linings are especially afflicted. Our creative brains easily gloss over possible pitfalls while focusing on the reward. We need Eeyore to counterbalance this natural propensity and keep us safe.

Anyone living with Eeyore should be careful about turning a deaf ear to his warnings. Although it may irritate us to the extreme, Eeyore's habit of pointing out flaws in our desires and poking holes in our dreams is sometimes one of his best gifts. While not every plan will unfold following the worst possible path, few people are able to see the roadblocks ahead when they are enamored by the journey. Eeyore can find the roadblocks because he has spent years concentrating on every possible bump.

Though the gift of balance Eeyore brings may not always

be accepted, it is difficult to miss. It is an in-your-face reality and an inescapable dynamic of the relationship. However, other gifts from Eeyore are more subtle. They are not self-evident, and sometimes they require a little searching to ferret out.

The Gift of Example

Grandma Bentley had been fearful all her life. Hundreds of small fears plagued her. Spiders, robbers, and fire were a few of the more consistent ones. But every decade or so, some new, big fear claimed the number one spot. The big fear always involved the most terrifying situation imaginable and was always something Grandma was totally helpless to prevent. This prime fear caused nightmares and consumed much of her energy during the day.

As a ten-year-old, her prime fear had been the threat of tornadoes. As a young mother, it was that Communists would take over America. When she turned fifty, it was the threat of cancer. Now, at seventy-two, it was the fear of spending her last days in a nursing home.

It should be noted that none of Grandma Bentley's fears were beyond possibility. These things might have happened. She was not psychotic or paranoid, just constantly focused on whatever she perceived to be the most painful possibility.

Her consistent fears left a few scars on her four children, but for the most part they grew up to be well-adjusted adults.

A large portion of this success was due to the balance provided by her ever-stable, low-key husband. The children gave birth to children of their own, and soon the clan numbered eighteen. Over time, the couple became the epitome of what grandparenting should be, and even their oldest child began referring to them as Grandma and Papa Bentley.

Then the world fell apart.

A heart attack bereaved the family of Papa, the father who had been their rock and fortress. The children all agreed they would be able to go on with life, but they seriously doubted how Grandma-the-Eeyore would manage the sudden death of the one who had stabilized and sheltered her for fifty years.

Alone in her home, Grandma went about the daily tasks of laundry, cooking, and feeding five cats. Physically, things seemed OK. Three of her children lived within ten miles of her front door, and the compact car she drove was nearly new. There wasn't much money, but with social security, a tiny savings account, and gifts from the children, she managed.

Then the fears came again.

Resurfacing like ghosts that refused to die, thoughts of spiders, robbers, and fire again made her heart race. The children recognized the symptoms. Whenever they visited her, these three fears drifted around the edge of most conversations. Finally, it was decided that Harold, the oldest, should speak with Grandma and find out how she was doing mentally.

Harold felt he had been shanghaied into this unwelcome assignment. What did being the oldest sibling have to do with talking to his mother about such things? His degree as a teacher had nothing to do with psychological stuff. The others were wrong; he had not been her favorite. One of the girls should have been sent on this unpleasant task, he thought.

When he rang the doorbell of the house where he had lived as a teen, he had no idea what he was going to say. Surely his mother would question why he had come without the family. He felt dumb and totally inadequate for what lay ahead.

However, the task proved far easier than he imagined. After a few awkward moments, his mother took the lead. She sensed that he had come about a serious concern, and she welcomed an honest discussion of what she was feeling and how she was managing life without Papa.

When she talked to Harold about her fear of fire and her fear that someone would break into the house during the night, her eyes misted and her hands shook. Harold inwardly sighed. Given the safety precautions that had been taken in her home and the low crime rate in her neighborhood, it was tempting to discount the fears as baseless, but he resisted the temptation. Harold just listened and waited.

It had been a long time since anyone had listened so patiently to her. It felt good, something like the security she had known before the death of her husband. After almost an hour of talk, she felt safe enough to confide her worst fear: spending her declining years in a nursing home.

Harold wanted to fix things for his mom, but he had no idea where to begin. Concerning the spiders, robbers, and fire, he wanted to tell her, "Don't be ridiculous. None of those things will happen!" But on the other hand, he had no way of predicting the future. He could no more offer an ironclad guarantee the house would never burn than he could absolutely assure her that she would never see the inside of a nursing home. He was back to feeling dumb and totally inadequate . . . and then he noticed something.

His mother always followed discussion of a fear with a "but." Yes, she was afraid of fire, but she refused to allow that fear to make her spend good money replacing current appliances for those without pilot lights. Yes, she worried about someone breaking into the house, but she was determined to sleep with her upstairs window open anyway. Yes, she feared a nursing home, but she didn't have that problem this week, and by God's good grace, she was determined not to cross that bridge until it was in front of her.

No matter how her voice quivered or how her eyes misted, it was evident that the woman everyone called Grandma intended to face the future head-on and battle the fears rather than giving in to them.

Harold reported to the clan that Grandma Bentley was capable of handling the future. However, it was what he did not report that made the biggest difference in his own life. He did not report on his own fears or what he had learned about managing them.

In his mother's eyes and the way she took a deep breath before adding "but," Harold found a true picture of courage.

51

From his perspective, spiders, robbers, and fire were very low on the list of worthy fears. Unreasonable school administrators, teenagers who didn't listen anymore, and rising mortgage payments were closer to the top.

But when he thought about it, he realized that it took as much courage for his mother to face her fear of a robber as it did for him to face the fear of the credit card debt that seemed to mount each month. Their emotional experiences were similar. So was the solution: Name the fear, and then face it. Don't run. And above all else, don't borrow trouble from tomorrow.

If we will carefully listen to Eeyore, we can come away with excellent examples for our own lives. Sometimes these examples will be of the extraordinary courage Eeyores occasionally express as they face such a negative world. Other times, the example will be how *not* to think and how to prevent letting molehills turn into mountains. Both examples are worthy gifts.

However, the gifts of Eeyore are not limited to balance and example. When we are willing to receive it, one of the best gifts may simply be a different way of viewing the world.

The Gift of Perspective

Not all Eeyores go from cradle to grave being followed by a dark cloud. Some visit Eeyore's Thistle Patch for a few months and then drift back to a more sunny meadow.

Jenise was only fifteen, but she had already cycled through the thistles twice. The first time was when she started her menstrual cycle in the fifth grade, and cramps kept this tomboy from pitching the final game of the season for the Mountain View Tigers. Becoming a woman under such adverse conditions put her in a resentful, mournful funk for nearly four months.

The second round came without any reason that could be identified by either parent or child. Three years of moderate sunshine had passed when, mysteriously, the dark cloud floated in one morning, and all the old negativism and hopelessness were back. At first, her mother feared they were in for another long siege, but about three weeks after the cloud arrived, it vanished as suddenly as it had come. Jenise still had moods and a tendency toward negative thinking, but these were brief and within expected bounds.

The third trip through the Thistle Patch came the summer after her junior year in high school. This time her always-patient mom, Liz, was wall-to-wall with other obligations and had little time or sympathy for the reluctance, moods, and sullen anger. She had just started a new job after eighteen years of stay-at-home mothering. Learning how to please her boss while still finding cracks in time to prepare meals and do laundry was harder than she'd thought it would be.

At first Liz didn't notice the change in her daughter. Jenise withdrew more often to her room, argued more with her brother, burst into tears for no reason, and generally behaved abominably—but Liz managed to ignore the storm warnings.

It wasn't until one Saturday evening when the house was quiet that she began to sense something was wrong. A quiet house on Saturday was just not normal.

Liz found her daughter in the last place on earth she expected—sitting on an old swing behind the oleander bushes. There were no tears. Jenise was just sitting there and appeared to be looking at nothing in particular.

"Is anything wrong?" Liz inquired. The responding grunt and shoulder shrug were followed by stoic silence. Liz recognized these signals as the teenage version of an open invitation to prod and pull.

Liz asked about Jenise's friend Tracy, whom she had not seen for a while. Jenise said that Tracy had gone to camp, but it didn't matter because she was tired of the relationship and didn't want her for a best friend anyway.

Liz countered with Proverbs 18:24, "A man of many companions may come to ruin, but there is a friend who sticks closer than a brother" (NIV). A mournful "Oh, mother" was followed by deafening silence.

Liz was tempted to turn back to the kitchen and leave Jenise to stew alone. But she realized that Jenise had been under the cloud for several weeks. This was not a passing mood, and her mother's heart wanted to fix her daughter's problem. Liz resisted the urge to leave and, instead, offered Jenise an alternative to the sleep/mope/sleep pattern she had seen developing.

"Would you like to attend Bible camp next month?" she asked.

Jenise said the camp was dumb and she wouldn't be caught dead there. Liz tried to cheer and encourage. She reminded Jenise that she had enjoyed the camp two years ago, and there was no way she could know that the camp would be "dumb" until she gave it a try. A verbal wall of "No way" blocked the idea.

By this point Liz was getting angry. At least she was trying to communicate. Jenise had to do her part. Liz changed tactics and tried a bit of guilt.

"You know I am working myself into the ground," Liz said. "If you are so bored with life, the least you could do is help with the yard. Your brother, Brian, is too little to push that mower, and your dad is working overtime."

Tears. "All you ever want me to do around here is work, work, work! You don't care!"

Liz gave up. This point/counterpoint debate was going nowhere. For a second time Liz had to resist the temptation to stomp off and let Jenise sulk. Instead, she sat down on a nearby tree stump and said nothing. She couldn't think of anything that was worth saying.

They sat in silence for several minutes. Liz's mind was empty of all thought. Arguing had sapped the last threads of her energy. Everything inside seemed a blank.

The blank faded into a strangely peaceful sadness as mother and daughter sat motionless. A distant bird took up a repetitive song. Without direction or effort, Liz's mind drifted from one subject to the next, like a stone thrown in slow motion skips over a pond: The reports she had been working on at the office would be due Tuesday. She had not finished last week's filing. Dinner would be pizza again. Her hip hurt. Maybe working was the wrong thing. Brian had a Little League game tonight at six. Life had been so much easier when the kids were young.

The thought caught her attention.

No, *she decided,* that's not quite true. *Those early years had had their own unique problems. Her mind drifted back. Crying babies. No money. Doing dumb stuff and feeling inadequate.*

Had life ever been carefree? Maybe before marriage and the kids? A vision of herself at seventeen floated to the surface. Bummer. Her parents moved that year. The pain had been almost palpable.

Liz looked across at her daughter sitting by the overgrown bushes. She remembered her as a three-year-old watching Sesame Street. Grover and Big Bird danced across the screen as background singers gave out with a snappy melody about big and little and how they change as one looks at the situation from a new perspective.

She was scarcely aware, but at that moment Liz received one small package containing an Eeyore gift: perspective. From Liz's viewpoint, her daughter's dark mood and obvious pain were caused by "little" things like summer boredom and a temporarily absent friend. It was ridiculous to waste so much energy brooding over such small stuff. But she remembered Big Bird and thought again.

Whether something was small or large depended on whose eyes were looking at it.

Liz let the idea of perspective soak a moment on her soul. What about her own current situation? New job. New schedule. New demands. Jenise would think these were very small when compared to missing her friend.

Eeyores dwell on the negative. They also tend to exaggerate small inconveniences and borrow possible problems from the future. This can be extremely irritating to the rest of us who have *real* things to worry about.

It can be very beneficial to pause for a moment. Eeyore feels the same burden, fear, and emotion over his concerns as we do over ours. When we're close to something, it looks big. When we view it from a distance, it seems small. It's all in the perspective. We can learn to empathize with Eeyore and see our own struggles from a new perspective if we will receive the gift Eeyore offers. Ultimately, we may even be able to view our current difficulties from the perspective of eternity. From that distance, *all* problems become small.

Receiving the gift of perspective almost always brings an inner feeling of hope and peace. But this is not true of all Eeyore's gifts. There are gifts that we desperately need, but they irritate us like fingernails scraping down a chalkboard! This is especially true of the most precious and eternal gifts.

The Gift of Eternal Reward

Peggy would have driven most people over the edge. Her deepest nature was not only the worst and most critical of all Eeyores, but in her old age she had become a demanding psychotic as well.

Peggy lived in the guest room of her son Frank's new home. Her arthritis had progressed to the point that she was nearly bedfast, a point that was hastened because she refused to endure any discomfort, including exercise, and demanded the right to eat what she wanted at anytime she pleased. Until her weary husband died, she had literally been waited on hand and foot by him. Now, her daughter-in-law inherited the unpleasant task of pleasing the bitter, old woman. Complicating the situation even further, Rachael also cared for her three-year-old daughter and nursing baby boy.

Peggy had a bell—a shrill, loud jangle that she rang with abandon anytime she wanted something. The TV channel needed changing. Ring! Her coffee was cold. Ring! She wanted to use the restroom. Ring! The grandchildren were too noisy. Ring, ring, RING! Day and night the bell summoned Rachael to her side, where she was expected to instantly supply all needs.

This intolerable situation had begun three years before with the death of Frank's father. He and Peggy were very wealthy, and before he died, he willed everything to his son with the provision that Peggy be cared for at home and never be institutionalized.

Motivated both by compassion and a need for financial security, Frank and Rachael agreed to the provisions of the will and now felt duty bound to keep the commitment.

There was not a person in the world who could be said to have liked Peggy. Even Frank barely tolerated her. While he could escape to his job, Rachael was trapped at home with demanding babies and the even more demanding bell.

Rachael was no supersaint. Every week she kept an appointment with her counselor, when she cried and poured out her weary, frustrated heart. Time after time she gave up and said she could not answer one more bell or listen to one more critical comment. But just as many times, she dried her tears and performed her duty.

What does a counselor say in a situation like that? We are trained to relieve pain and find solutions to life's problems. That is why people pay us. But what about the times when there are no solutions and the pain cannot be avoided?

In times like that I am grateful the insurance companies list one of my specialties as Christian counseling. Through that grid, I can offer real hope, hope centered on the foundation of biblical truths. The most important truth I will ever teach anyone comes through helping my clients clearly see a sovereign God and the reality of life everlasting. That truth transcends even the worst circumstance and provides peace.

Ever since Eden, mankind has struggled under the burden

of judgment. Humans wanted the right to judge good and evil, and we got what we wanted (see Genesis 3:1-7). Now, when we face painful circumstances, our first reaction is to resist the inequity of it all and plead that life is not fair and God can't be good, or he would never allow a particular thing.

The surprising thing is, if we look at life only from earth's view, that judgment is absolutely right. If we do as Solomon suggested in Ecclesiastes and consider only what is under the sun, the conclusion can never be anything but a sorrowful admission that all is empty, senseless, and unfair. Yet, lifting our eyes to view circumstances from Heaven's perspective is impossible because earth is all we have ever known.

But it is precisely the heavenly perspective we must have if we are to be at peace with painful circumstances. It takes God's revelation—usually through his Word but sometimes in other ways—to show us things outside earth and beyond time. The more real these eternal, spiritual truths become, the more we will rest in the midst of confusion, the more hope we will have even while pain endures. And through it all, the more we will look forward with true expectation to that wonderful day when we'll hear, "Well done, good and faithful servant; you were faithful over a few things, I will make you ruler over many things" (Matthew 25:21).

There are realities beyond this world. There are rewards worth having that transcend time and space. In Matthew 10:42, Jesus assured us that every time we reach beyond ourselves to offer so much as a cup of cold water to someone because we are his servant, that act will be rewarded. There is a time when we will know that the judge of all the earth has always done what is right.

If relationship with other humans provides an opportunity to earn eternal rewards, then relationship with an Eeyore offers even more opportunity. And relationship with someone like Peggy must set the cash registers of Heaven spinning!

Receiving the Gifts

The gifts of Eeyore may not come wrapped in brightly colored paper or be purchased at a store, but they *are* real gifts. And like all gifts, the offerings of Eeyore must be recognized, received, and owned before they can benefit us.

I was at a conference where I admired a large bouquet on the speaker's table. Several times I remarked about the lovely blooms. At the end of the conference, I was told the bouquet had been purchased as a gift for me. The flowers were originally something I'd admired from afar. Now they'd become an enormous object I would have to transport home. The entire dynamic involving the uncooperative, delicate, wet gift changed. Within seconds I went from admiration to appreciation to grief! It is possible not to recognize a gift and even possible to be reluctant to receive one!

Gifts from Eeyore are like that. They are easily overlooked and even more easily rejected.

Do you want to find peace while you live with your Eeyore? Search for the gifts. He may not know he is giving them, and you may find yourself reluctant to receive them. But what Eeyore offers are true gifts just the same. Being willing to recognize the gifts and open ourselves before God to receive them is a challenge. But once accomplished, the process is guaranteed to enrich our lives.

There can be many reasons why gifts are rejected, but anger and pride are the most common. These unlovely character traits have caused people to turn down fantastic gifts in the physical world. Most of us have known people in deep financial need who turned down assistance because their pride would not let them admit anything was wrong. I remember a mother who refused to accept the offer of love and relationship from her adult daughter because angry memories of the girl's rebellious past kept getting in the way.

If we can reject gifts that are so clear and immediate, how easy can it be to accept gifts from Eeyore, gifts that may be much more abstract and spiritual in nature?

Anger may be the most common reason Eeyore's gifts are pushed away. If we resent and resist a particular relationship as a whole, the gifts seem unacceptable. Human nature not only demands that my anger be allowed, but that self and others recognize my anger as a good (justified) thing to feel. Accepting gifts throws a monkey wrench into the machinery of justification.

Pride is another common reason for resistance. Accepting the gift may obligate us to the giver. We so much enjoy the feeling of being superior to our particular Eeyores, we don't want to see the benefit they are to our lives. In that kind of situation, gifts are an intolerable nuisance.

Some people have simply fallen into a habit of resistance. Their first reaction to anything is *no, not now,* or *not me.* Reactions like these may indicate we have a few Eeyoreish tendencies of our own! But those who are willing to open their hearts and accept the gifts Eeyore offers have the wonderful privilege of using those things for their own pleasure and benefit.

I'll admit that I would find it easier to enjoy the gift of a new car than to enjoy balance, example, perspective, and even eternal reward. Shame on me. That demonstrates how far I am from seeing things as God sees them. It is not that the Almighty would frown on my enjoyment of a new car—only that cars, houses, land, money, and even physical bodies will pass into decay. How much more valuable are eternal things like character, God's approval, and heavenly reward.

Want to really delight, as well as confuse, your Eeyore? Think of a gift from Eeyore that has recently come your way. Hug his neck and say thank you. You don't need to say exactly what you are thanking him for (that might shed more heat than light on the relationship), but a hug and sincere appreciation can make even an old donkey smile.

> GET THE POINT

When a problem person enters your life, looking for the good can make the trial less severe.

> > READ THE BOOK

Look up 1 Thessalonians 5:18.

1. Why should we be thankful?

2. What are the things for which we are not to be thankful?

Check out Revelation 2:2, 9, 13, 19; 3:1, 8, 15.

1. Jesus told seven churches that he knew things about them. What are some of those things? Which of them would Jesus say are true of you?

2. During hard times it is tempting to feel alone and think no one knows the severity of your trials. Could realizing that Jesus knows these things about you bring comfort? How do you think his statements made those who originally received his letter feel?

Examine Philippians 4:8, 9.

1. If you spend your time thinking on the positive things Paul lists here, what will be the result?

2. Verse 8 says to "meditate" on those things. What would that involve?

> > > TELL THE TRUTH

1. Describe a time when you benefited because of something painful that entered your life.

2. The gifts of Eeyore discussed in this chapter have mostly centered on painful things, but Eeyore has other gifts too. List five positive character qualities possessed by your personal Eeyore that are qualities you easily enjoy. (Examples: She is an excellent pianist. He is a faithful provider.)

3. What would likely happen if you chose a good quality possessed by Eeyore and told him or her about it this week?

CHAPTER FOUR

━ • • • • • ━

Listening to Eeyore

"Why, what's the matter?" [asked Pooh].

"Nothing, Pooh Bear, nothing. We can't all, and some of us don't. That's all there is to it."

"Can't all what?" said Pooh, rubbing his nose.

"Gaiety. Song-and-dance. Here we go round the mulberry bush."

Living with Eeyore can be a bit like living by a railroad track. After a while you stop hearing the train. This is good because filtering obnoxious noise is a natural defense that keeps us sane. It is also bad because if we don't listen to Eeyore, we will never form a genuine relationship or benefit from his gifts.

So amid the roar and the rattle, how do we hear the negativity without developing calloused ears? How often can one listen to the rhetoric of misery without becoming pretty miserable as well? Is there a way to listen—really listen—without drowning in despair?

Maybe.

It's a tough balancing act, but listening without being overwhelmed is a skill that can be learned. The problem is, the skill is only taught via on-the-job training. You have to be in relationship with Eeyore and be hearing what you don't want to hear before you can practice. The process is a little like learning to swim when the boat just sank and you have no other choice.

Negative information will always be flowing from Eeyore. That is unavoidable.

Artists see vivid colors in fog and starlight. Preachers find sermon illustrations when they go to the market for oranges. Mathematicians notice a formula that will explain the pattern of the tiles on the ceiling.

Eeyores find flaws.

The process is as natural as breathing.

Yes, I'm Listening!

Most of us fall into one of two categories. Neither of these is the category of a listener. We either express and defend, or we grow deaf and ignore. Ears are common, but finding someone who listens is rare.

Eeyores bring even more complications to this already complex dynamic. Eeyores point out flaws, but they seldom struggle under the burden of needing to act. When others listen to Eeyore, they feel pressure to do something, fix something, or change something. Eventually, these negative comments become a load strapped to their backs. Listening to Eeyore can make one very tired.

The trick we must learn is to really listen—and convince Eeyore that we *are* listening—while at the same time shrugging off loads of guilt, gloom, and responsibility that are not properly our own. The best advice I can give is to suggest we use the LRE plan of action: Look. Reflect. Escape. When we *look* and *reflect,* we learn to listen in a way that emotionally satisfies Eeyore. When we *escape,* we protect ourselves from being overwhelmed by a burden that is heavier than we want to bear. Escaping doesn't minister to Eeyore, but it is a safety valve that keeps us sane!

L *Is for Looking*

At a conference for counselors, I heard author Gary Collins tell a story about his four-year-old daughter.

He had come home tired and immediately sought out his easy chair and newspaper. However, his little daughter had other plans and was anxious to tell him about her day. She stood on one side of the chair, chattering while he responded with grunts and occasional comments. She stood on the other side of the chair and repeated the same statements. Again, he verbally responded while keeping his vision glued to the paper before him. Finally, the exasperated little girl stood directly in front of him. She put her tiny hand on the top of the paper and crushed it into her father's lap, saying, "No, Daddy. You must listen to me with your eyes!"

She had a good point. Humans need eye contact so they know they are being heard.

Not listening to some people will cause them to talk less. Not listening to an Eeyore may make him talk more. If you have lived by the train so long that its noise no longer impacts you, it might be time to change your ways. Listening—really listening—to someone for thirty minutes can satisfy both parties in a way that two hours by the train track never will. And a satisfied Eeyore is a lot easier to live with.

Remember, listening begins with the eyes. *L* is for looking.

R *Is for Reflecting*

Although eye contact may be the number one way of helping someone feel heard, a very close runner-up is repeating back what you just heard him or her say. That may seem a bit strange, but it works. It's hard to argue with success. I had to go to school a long time to learn the skill. I'll give it to you in a few paragraphs, and you don't have to register for school or pay a dime!

Graduate school is never easy; but when you attempt it during midlife, things are really hairy. And I had the additional complications of widowhood and teenage children. Among the many theoretical approaches I had to learn, one was called client-centered therapy, using the techniques of Carl Rogers.

The basic procedure is simple. A client talks, and the counselor listens for two things: content and emotion. Having heard these two things, the therapist then uses the client's own words to repeat back what he heard. Then he watches the response of the client to see if he assessed correctly. He doesn't solve problems. He doesn't offer corrections or ideas. He doesn't do anything. He is simply totally present with the client, patiently listening and reflecting.

Frankly, I thought the whole concept sounded suspicious. It seemed a little deceptive to expect someone to pay me good money so that I could sit across the desk and repeat back what had just been told to me. However, teachers assured me that clients would not only pay, they would leave my office feeling satisfied and happy.

I could not understand how such a simple thing could possibly work, but I had a sixteen-year-old daughter who was driving me batty, so I thought I would give the process a try.

Every evening Nancy bounced into my bedroom and unloaded her frustrations about the cheerleading squad. Nancy was captain and determined that her squad would win the upcoming competition. Every evening I offered suggestions for fixing her problems. Every evening she flounced out the bedroom complaining, "You never listen to me." I had nothing to lose by attempting Rogers's way of doing things.

The next night was the same as always. Nancy bounced into the bedroom and complained, "You will never believe what Cindy did today! She forgot her uniform again. I had to make the whole squad wait twenty minutes while her mother brought it from home. If she were my kid, I would have slapped her!"

I had a dozen replies ready on my tongue. I wanted to suggest that instead of making the entire squad wait, Nancy give Cindy twenty minutes on the bench while the others continued to practice. I wanted to tell her to be a little more forgiving and that good parents didn't slap kids. Instead, I obeyed Rogers and assessed what I had just heard.

Content: Cindy forgot uniform.

Emotion: anger.

I said something like, "So, Cindy forgot her uniform again, and that really made you angry." Then I shut my mouth and waited to see if I had reflected correctly. According to my teachers, if I hit the nail on the head, it would immediately be evident. Either Nancy's nonverbal expressions would show agreement, or she would talk at a deeper level.

Both happened. Her face brightened, she seemed to relax, and her words flowed like a river. I offered nothing significant to this one-sided conversation, but a few times when she drew a breath or seemed to be experiencing a strong feeling, I reflected the content and emotion I thought I heard.

Half an hour later Nancy bounced happily out of my room. She paused at the door and looked back. "Mom," she said slowly, "we had such a good conversation tonight. Thanks for listening."

Conversation? What conversation? Both parties have to talk before it is a conversation. As for listening, I had been listening night after night for weeks! The difference was not in my hearing. The difference was that for the first time Nancy *knew* I was listening.

Being able to solve problems and give good advice are excellent qualities. And hearing what another person is saying is important. But none of those things will make a difference to Eeyore unless he *knows* you are listening. Being able to convince another that you have heard and understood what he is trying to tell you is foundational. Until that happens, no real communication can be built.

Additionally, if your Eeyore is of the verbal variety and feels that you have not heard, he may try to make you understand by repeating the same negative comments again and again. Perhaps you heard it the first time, but until

Eeyore makes an emotional connection with the fact that you heard, the train will keep passing by. Closing your ears only prolongs the rumble.

R is for reflecting. It can be the best way ever invented for stopping a train.

E *Is for Escaping*

When engaged in any risky venture—such as scuba diving, landing a spaceship, or boarding a commercial flight to New York—it is wise to locate the escape hatches in advance of need. Relationships are also risky ventures, especially relationship with an Eeyore. Therefore, it just makes good sense to plan your escape route in advance of need—and not be ashamed of using it.

When Eeyore's cloud gets too oppressive, find a way to run. Go to a friend. Walk in the park. Take in a movie. Go to your room and knit. It really doesn't matter what you do, as long as the action accomplishes what is intended. You need rest and an opportunity to regain balance. Take it.

Having a few well-thought-out escape hatches prepared in advance and using them judiciously can be a lifesaver. It is good for you, and it is good for Eeyore too. There is more about the art of escaping at the end of this chapter, but for now, here is a checklist of four don'ts to observe before you flee.

Don't feel guilty. As long as you have demonstrated a willingness to listen and you have a commitment to stay in relationship, a brief time away is nothing to feel guilty about.

Don't tempt yourself. When you plan your escape, make sure that it does not involve things that may lead to sin. For example, it is not a good idea to go shopping in the mall when Eeyore nags about the rising credit card debt. If you are a man, it is not a good idea to escape by going to the apartment of an old girlfriend so you can vent about your wife's critical attitudes. The same advice goes for females and old boyfriends. Those who refuse to use common sense when planning escape routes will pay for their stupidity.

Don't stay gone. No one can tell you how long your escape should take. At the end of the previous chapter, we discussed the tragic situation of Rachael and bell-ringing Peggy. Rachael escaped from the house twice each week— once for a one-hour counseling appointment and once for two hours of shopping while a sitter took care of Peggy. She also escaped for one hour each night while enjoying a long, undisturbed bath. For that one hour, Frank held the fort. She never abused these privileges and always returned on time.

Don't avoid Eeyore altogether. Escape hatches are intended for brief respite, a time to strengthen body and soul. God has put Eeyore in your path for specific reasons. Don't miss the gifts that could have been yours. Be very careful to put as much effort into listening as you do into escaping.

Oh yes, and above all else, tell your Eeyore that you are checking out and when you will be back. If you don't tell Eeyore you are gone, he may keep talking to the wall. This perpetuates the train syndrome and makes matters worse. If you don't tell Eeyore when you will be back, you discourage an already discouraged individual and foster hopelessness. Giving notice of abdication and schedule of return is simply common manners.

Listening to your Eeyore can be difficult when he finds fault with the politicians, the weather, and his own gall bladder.

But listening at this level is child's play when compared to the difficulty of listening when Eeyore points out the flaws in *you*. At that point, the rain of negative comment turns into the stinging hailstones of criticism.

The Hailstones of Criticism

When Eve decided it would be a good thing to judge between right and wrong on her own terms, a fundamental change took place in all mankind. Our first parents wanted the right to judge; now none of us can avoid it. Children start judging as soon as they can talk. One of the first phrases out of their mouths will be "It's not fair!" Humans judge everything from the proper way to cook steak to moral absolutes. When we verbalize our judgments, it is called criticism.

As Stacy got ready for work, she was frustrated and angry. She had been married only six months, and her husband was quickly becoming more of a father than a companion. They had been warned in premarital classes about the parent/child pattern that couples can drift into. But she couldn't for the life of her remember how they said to fix it!

It was only 7:43 AM, and she had already been criticized, corrected, or reminded fifteen times! She knew the number was correct. She had counted.

She was told she should have set the alarm for six rather than six fifteen. Her skirt was too short. She must be careful to remember their dinner engagement with the Smiths; wasn't it cute that blondes were so forgetful? Was she putting on a few pounds? Taking lunch would be so much better than buying it. Did she take her birth control pill?

On and on and on. Why couldn't John see that his constant criticism did nothing to make her feel cared for and loved? It was driving her away. Why couldn't he just keep his mouth shut?

There are basic reasons why people criticize. Understanding a few of them may help you balance the criticism and discern how to respond to the onslaught. Much could be said on the subject, but I offer three possible sources: criticism rooted in pride, criticism rooted in fear, and criticism rooted in anger—serving the purpose of revenge.

Criticism Based in Pride

I believe the most common reason for criticism is because we are all too much like the Ford Motor Company. We are convinced that we have a better idea, and we foolishly assume that if we verbalize our wisdom, intelligent creatures will thank us and mend the error of their ways.

It never happens, but we keep on believing that it someday will!

One definition of *insanity* is "when someone does the same thing over and over again but keeps expecting the results to be different." In this regard, we are all a bit nuts. We repeat the same behavior over and over while expecting the results miraculously to change one day.

Need proof? Is there anyone left on the planet who has not acted as though he could drink, eat, smoke, drive, or behave however he wanted and suffer no health consequences?

When John criticized Stacy, he kept expecting her to thank him and change. He tenaciously held on to that belief while ignoring both facts and past experience. Because he believed in the wisdom and rightness of his own judgments, he thought if he said something loud enough and long enough, the mountain would finally give way and move to the sea.

As you listen to your Eeyore, recognize that much of the verbal onslaught you feel comes from an honest desire to help make you "better." That realization won't solve the problem, but it might ease your pain a bit, helping you separate the behavior of criticism from bad character. Eeyore probably thinks he is benefiting you!

One idea for managing a problem like Stacy's is for the partners to agree on the number of personal corrections that are allowed each day. Chances are John does not even realize how often he corrects, advises, and mentions flaws. Having John's permission to point out each time she feels criticized may help Stacy control the situation.

At this point, in fairness to readers, I must insert a strong warning. When attempting this exercise, there is one ground rule that must be very clear and always observed. The issue is what you *feel*, not what Eeyore intended or even the significance of the flaw. Above all else, don't get drawn into a discussion about whether it was a "real" criticism or a "normal" comment. It doesn't matter which is true. Your *feelings* about the remark are what is being counted, not how Eeyore intended the words to sound or how much the correction was needed.

Once the ground rules are clear, count aloud every time you feel criticized. But don't be surprised if your Eeyore keeps count on you too. This exercise might be an eye-opener for both of you.

Of course, your efforts at control may fall flat, but the exercise is worth a try. Just remember that you will never change Eeyore's critical nature by criticizing *him*. If you have already pointed out his critical nature fifty-six times, and he is just as critical as ever, stop. The mountain won't move by your efforts. Accept that fact and quit wasting your energy.

Criticism Based in Fear

Another motivation for criticism is fear. I suspect many Eeyores are either born with fear-filled personalities or have gone through childhood experiences that created unusual fear. This may explain the hypervigilance that keeps Eeyore expecting the worst. Being fearful for someone you love can make critical comments fall out of your mouth.

Molly was an Eeyore. This fact was most often demonstrated in the way she related to her adult daughter, Tiffany. Molly constantly pointed out flaws and felt a pressure to help fix the problems she perceived, but Tiffany resisted her efforts.

Tiffany brought the situation to a head when she told her mother she had to have more respect and space if the relationship were to continue. At the top of the list of things that had to change were Molly's calls that often came three and four times a day. Tiffany simply could not take one more correction via phone tag.

Molly wanted to comply with the request. The idea of anything—even herself—interfering with her relationship with her only child was terrifying, and she promised Tiffany that she would change. Five times that week she had put down the phone

81

when she wanted to call and check on things. It was Wednesday, and she had called only four times in the week!

However, Tiffany was going to register little April for kindergarten tomorrow, and Molly knew she would forget to take the birth certificate. Edging toward the bedroom phone, she stopped and pulled back her hand.

In her mind's eye she could see Tiffany's embarrassment before the school officials when she came to the registration unprepared. Her husband, Paul, would likely get angry if the deadline were missed. April would cry if she could not attend opening day. Tiffany was going to be in pain. Molly had to help her. She picked up the phone and dialed the number. Fear had triumphed over Molly's good sense and best intentions.

One way love expresses itself is by warning the beloved of danger. God himself pleads, cautions, and instructs his own. Love seeks to protect.

The difference between God and Eeyore is that the Almighty knows all sides of the issue and is motivated by a desire for our advancement. Sometimes, letting us struggle a bit with personal inadequacies or letting us face an embarrassment is good for strengthening our characters. But Eeyore can never lay aside his personal fear long enough to consider a loved one's long-term good.

The story is told of a compassionate farmer who looked out the kitchen window and saw a butterfly struggling to escape the chrysalis that bound her. In an effort to help, the farmer took a knife and split open the cocoon. Within moments the butterfly dropped to the earth dead. Without a time of struggle to strengthen her wings, she could not live.

Eeyores are sometimes too compassionate for the good of their loved ones.

There is not a lot you can do if your Eeyore is motivated by fear. Occasionally, discussing the dynamics with him may be of some benefit, but more than likely the warnings, corrections, and criticisms will remain as long as Eeyore's fear-based love.

Criticism Based in Anger (Revenge)

A third motivation for criticism is anger rooted in a desire for revenge and control. Frequently this takes the form of sarcasm, or it can sound like sticky-sweet sentimentalism. This kind of criticism is the ultimate I-don't-get-mad-I-get-even weapon, for it can be thrown with such subtlety that the target is destroyed while the attacker is free to take the high moral ground.

The book of Proverbs tells how a fool hurts another person and then refuses to take responsibility for the pain he has inflicted: "Like a madman who throws firebrands, arrows, and death, is the man who deceives his neighbor, and says, 'I was only joking!'" (Proverbs 26:18, 19). When we throw verbal barbs, jokes that hide cutting remarks, two-sided statements with hidden meanings, and innuendos . . . then blame the other person for becoming upset, we are playing the part of the fool and acting like a madman. If an Eeyore in your life is expert at this destructive game, you know the helplessness, anger, and confusion as you feel these missiles come crashing into your soul while Eeyore puts the blame on you for misunderstanding or being too sensitive.

Gratefully, not too many Eeyores go as far as Anthony's dad, but reading his example may help you identify a less severe pattern in your own relationship.

Anthony didn't hate his father. He just avoided him like cancer. Most of the time Anthony could talk his wife into the weekly visits to Rolling Hills Nursing Home. But she had flatly refused to go on Father's Day. Anthony needed to personally deliver the card she had bought. What kind of son was he if he wouldn't even wish a happy holiday to the man who gave him life?

When he pulled into the parking lot, his stomach did a flip. When he walked up the steps, he felt like he was ten years old and coming home late. When he entered the room, guilt and inadequacy hung around him like the chains of a ghost from the story of Ebenezer Scrooge.

"Well, if it isn't Little Tony come to see his dying old man." The voice came from the chair in the corner of the room where his father sat watching the omnipresent TV.

Anthony winced. He had always hated being called Little Tony, and his father knew it. From another father the statement might have been a tease, but Anthony knew his father never joked.

"You're such a busy man," his father continued. "Your mother, bless her soul, would be grateful you found the time to stop by."

They had played this game before. His father was angry. Cutting his son with barbed remarks was a way of getting even. Only last week Anthony's wife had told his father things were slow at the company. As for Anthony's mother, his father hated her and had divorced the woman when Anthony was only a young boy.

Anthony could feel the anger coming from the other side of the room. Each phrase was a spear intended to punish and produce guilt. But if Anthony challenged his father or responded with an anger of his own, his father would increase the guilt by claiming that his words had been normal, loving statements that any caring father might say.

True Eeyores are almost never mean. But Anthony's father was mean. And mean individuals can adopt Eeyore's ways. When they do, the combination of evil, depression, and statements with double meaning can make anyone who must stay in relationship with them want to run.

While Anthony's example may be a bit extreme, it is not at all unusual for critical statements to be motivated by revenge. Because criticism is Eeyore's native language, it is easy for his anger to find its expression via that medium.

When Eeyore has offered you his wisdom (criticism based in pride) and warned you because he cares (criticism based in fear), and yet your behavior hasn't changed, his critical comments will likely increase—if for no other reason than Eeyore is royally ticked off.

It is at times like these when listening becomes a real chore.

Two Key Defenses

Criticism itself is not a bad thing. We all need correction now and then. Well-thought-out and lovingly delivered criticism can correct, enlighten, and promote change for the better. It can remove flaws and protect when someone is headed in the wrong direction. The problem comes when the product is overused. Like salt, a little criticism goes a long way. Too much will make you sick. Unfortunately, Eeyores seldom seem to understand that principle. So I close this chapter about listening to Eeyore by offering a couple of defense tactics.

Defense #1: Surround Yourself with Positives

Through the use of very small instruments that record such things as hand temperature, muscle tension, and breath rate, researchers can measure the discomfort a person feels. This procedure allows the researchers to accurately compare a person's response to negative vs. positive statements. The data are in, and the results are clear: it takes *ten positive statements* to counterbalance the discomfort caused by one critical comment.

Can you imagine how much positive input it would take to restore harmony after the negative statements your Eeyore made to you just this morning? Where are you going to get all that positive feedback? Like the Little Red Hen, you may find that you have to do the job yourself.

Ideas abound for keeping positive input in your day, but you must be the one to initiate and make it happen. Place a joke of the day on your computer desktop, or use a calendar in which every page contains an encouraging idea. Each morning read a devotion from *Our Daily Bread* or something similar. (Choose from an assortment of devotional books by visiting www.standardpub.com.) Or you might want to order a monthly short story of encouragement sent to your computer. You can sign up on my Web site www. ElizabethBakerBooks.com. You could keep a ring binder of encouraging cards and notes that people have sent you through the years. Get a pet. Make a game out of finding ten things each day for which you can feel grateful. Memorize Scriptures that are uplifting and encouraging. Play happy music.

You can't always avoid negative comments, but you do have a choice about some of the positives that surround you. Don't depend on Eeyore for all your sunshine. Manufacture a bit of your own.

Defense #2: Run Away . . . but Don't Go Far

Social researchers enjoy naming groups of people. Each generation even seems to need a special identification. There are the Builders and Boomers and Busters and others. In some textbooks, the Me generation of the late '80s is also known as the Peter Pan generation—a group who insist that they will never grow up.

Please don't take my encouragement to escape as an excuse for irresponsibility. Escape hatches are intended for occasional use and only when remaining where you are is guaranteed to make things worse, not better. Escape hatches were never intended as pleasure trips for Peter Pan. Because God is using Eeyore to give gifts and sharpen your character, don't be too quick to run.

On the other hand, there is no medal of sainthood awarded for exposing yourself to unnecessary pain and no biblical requirement to live without rest and refreshment. When have you listened enough and it is time for a break? Who makes the decision of when to patiently nod and when to retreat? You do.

Although that is a responsibility that, if taken seriously, could keep you up at night, rest assured that God is not out to get you—even if it may seem at times as though Eeyore is. If you have an honest heart, stay in the Word, and want a healthy balance, God will help you know the right thing to do, even if there is an occasional stumble along the way.

> GET THE POINT

Being a good listener to a critical Eeyore is not easy, but with wisdom it can be done.

> > READ THE BOOK

Read James 1:19, 20.

1. We are not responsible for the actions of others, but we ourselves should always be eager to listen well. Why does James say that?

2. Do these verses indicate that anger is always wrong?

Delve into 1 Corinthians 4:12, 13; 2 Corinthians 6:4-10.

1. In 1 Corinthians, what was the example Paul left us when he was criticized falsely?

89

2. In 2 Corinthians, Paul says that when confronted with trouble and persecution, he and the others on his team "commended" themselves. What were some ways in which they did that?

Check out Titus 3:2; Ephesians 4:31, 32.

1. What things do these references say should characterize a Christian's speech? What things should *not?*

Study 2 Samuel 16:5-13.

1. At the lowest point in David's life, Shimei added to his troubles by pouring hurtful, critical words on him. What was David's response?

2. How does Romans 12:21 apply to the situation David faced?

>>> TELL THE TRUTH

1. Is it ever necessary to take a tough stand against critical words? If so, when?

2. Have you ever known a situation in which it was better to withdraw than to continue trying to communicate? Describe it.

CHAPTER FIVE

Talking to Eeyore

"There is an invitation . . . asking you to the party. Tomorrow."

Eeyore shook his head slowly.

"You mean Piglet. The little fellow with the excited ears. That's Piglet. I'll tell him."

"No, no!" said Owl, getting quite fussy. "It's you!"

"Are you sure?"

"Of course I'm sure. Christopher Robin said, 'All of them! Tell all of them.'"

"All of them, except Eeyore?"

"All of them," said Owl sulkily.

"Ah!" said Eeyore. "A mistake, no doubt, but still, I shall come. Only don't blame me if it rains."

T here is only one task more difficult than listening to Eeyore: talking to him. At least when one is listening, success of the project depends on one's self. When talking, success depends on a response from the other side. You can't control that.

Pastor Max Casslin left the elders' board meeting frustrated, discouraged, and ready to resign. Every idea he brought up, every solution he offered, every long-term dream he mentioned had been shot down and picked apart by his lead elder, Scott Brown.

When Max accepted the pastoral position last year, he thought Scott might become a friend as well as an asset on the board of elders. They had a lot in common, and Max was delighted by Scott's dry wit and knowledge of the Scriptures. Max never understood why their budding friendship withered, but he did know that no matter what he said or how long he talked, Scott could not catch his vision and the deep confidence he felt for the future of Calvary Church. No matter how hard Max tried, Scott just couldn't get it. That inability was blocking the entire progress of the church, and Max feared it would one day kill the work God had begun.

There are many possibilities in a situation like the one Max faced, but one strong possibility is that Scott is an Eeyore by nature. Given time, Max might find that Scott is more on board and supportive than his negative responses indicate.

It is the nature, and at times the gift, of Eeyore to see and hear everything through a dark filter. Because of this mind-set, facts get shaded and hopes get ignored. When Eeyore verbalizes the impressions he's getting, everyone around him feels unheard. Getting facts and dreams beyond Eeyore's filter can be quite a challenge.

One thing's for certain: you are not going to fundamentally change an Eeyore. Expect the negative responses and slow acceptance of anything new. If you try to force Eeyore into becoming a positive personality, you are guaranteed to lose before you begin.

You can't pull off Eeyore's negative filters, but knowing the filters are there and allowing Eeyore to express himself according to what he perceives as truth can be the first steps to getting your own message through.

Eeyores move slowly, and Tiggers bounce fast. When they try to do anything together—as in sharing seats on a committee or making a marriage work—both parties are guaranteed to need an abundant supply of time and mutual grace.

Even under the best of circumstances, communication is not easy. Communicating with Eeyore is more difficult still. But don't despair. If your attempts at conversation end up sounding like dialogue from a Three Stooges movie or Abbott and Costello doing their routine of "Who's on First?" a few well-honed skills applied with perseverance may unclog the pipeline and get things moving again.

Defense Tactics

The negative ear filters that Eeyore wears are a basic part of his unique temperament. Expect them. If he didn't have them, he wouldn't be an Eeyore! However, there are other, less flattering elements that mess up communication, and your Eeyore probably has his share of them. These are not pure idiosyncrasy of personality but ugly stuff that looks more like remnants of fallen Adam.

The biggest ear stopper we all struggle against is our desire to defend ourselves against the success of another. We don't just want a solution; we want *our* solution. We don't want to have a conversation; we want others to *listen*. We don't want simply to get our way; we want others to *agree* that our way is best! This is a tragic analysis of the human condition, but true nonetheless.

One way this self-protective, self-promoting instinct works its way out into conversation is through secondary gains. Few of us are smart enough to use these defenses with consciously applied skill, but we don't have to. Our powerful, conniving, creative brains are fully capable of doing these things for us automatically!

Secondary Gains

Bonnie had been admitted with an eating disorder to the psych unit where I worked. Her bulimia threatened to rupture her esophagus, destroy her teeth, and stop her heart from beating. *It was obvious to all the staff and even the other patients that Bonnie was deeply angry with her husband. Throwing up until her life was threatened was one way she got even with him. She also evened the score by riding the clutch in their van. The clutch had been replaced three times, creating huge arguments and expense. The last time tension over replacing the clutch escalated, Bonnie ended up in the hospital.*

Bonnie couldn't put any of this together. Driving with her foot resting on the clutch was an unconscious habit. It wasn't her fault. It meant nothing. She never intended to destroy the van. After all, Bonnie was a Christian. She never got angry, and she certainly wouldn't seek revenge on her perfect-in-every-way husband.

During a group session, Bonnie was again being challenged to look at her behavior in the light of anger. Suddenly she turned to the person next to her and started hitting the fellow patient with her fist while shouting, "I am not angry!"

As staff jumped from their chairs to stabilize the situation, Bonnie suddenly stopped and looked at her balled fist; then she burst into tears. Could she possibly be angry? Could seeking revenge on her husband be part of her problem? Staff had been telling her this for a week, but she couldn't hear a word we said while her stubborn self-defenses blockaded the way. She needed to get even with her husband but at the same time guard her reputation as the nearly perfect wife of a totally perfect man. Her creative brain found a way to let her get everything she wanted.

People of all personality types experience being motivated by secondary gains. Sometimes motives are so deeply buried that we are shocked when circumstances or the Holy Spirit reveals our true intent. At other times, we are dimly aware of our deepest motivation, but we rationalize and argue with ourselves until we deceive our own minds. Then the self-centered reason for our behavior retreats into the shadows of the subconscious.

While we all experience behavior motivated by secondary gains, Eeyore's secondary gains often take on a peculiar slant that is a unique expression of his personality. When Eeyore's gloomy predictions turn out to be right, he gains the illusion of being ahead of the game, in the know, and safely in control. Besides, even Eeyore enjoys a good "I told you so" every once in a while.

Another expression of secondary gains that often bears a distinctly Eeyore imprint is risk avoidance. Resisting encouragement and being deaf to positive pleading can provide a perverse kind of safety. If there is no chance for Eeyore to succeed, then there is no reason for him to try. And if he never tries, he can never fail. Circular reasoning? Yes, but it works if you're an Eeyore!

Amanda was not exceptionally pretty, she struggled with shyness, her grades were average, and her family was not well off. But she had one obvious talent: she could play the flute like a budding prodigy. Her mother tried to tell her that she could win a college scholarship with this talent. Her band director continually encouraged her to challenge the section leader for first chair.

Both of these encouragements fell on deaf ears. Amanda always had excuses for not taking action. She hadn't practiced enough. She would never be the best. She forgot the music. If all else failed, she melted into tears and moaned, "You just don't understand."

The truth was that Amanda was an Eeyore, and her only safety was in not trying, not competing, and not hearing the encouraging words all around her. Deep inside she was terrified of freezing up in a contest. Even if she did win first chair, she feared all the other students would hate her for being the best. If she tried, there was a chance she might fail. That would be the ultimate horror. As long as she refused to hear about the possibilities of success, she was safe.

If you suspect your Eeyore's dull ears are stopped with a secondary gain, your only course of action is to gently, persistently bring what you see to his attention. Because secondary gains are by definition an unconscious process, realize you are dealing with an area about which only God can be certain. Be humble enough to recognize that you may be wrong. Suggest to Eeyore that there is a connection between the secondary gain he will receive and his stubborn refusal to listen to reason. Then leave the results to the Holy Spirit.

Shifting Subjects

The list of all possible secondary gains would be as long as a list of all human desires and fears. Covering a territory that large would be more than the author wants to write or the reader wants to process. But I think it would be profitable to look at one of the more common secondary gains, one that is infamous for clogging up the machinery of communication: the fine art of shifting the subject.

It was one in the morning. Brenda and Clint had been arguing for five hours, and they were no closer to a solution than they had been at eight that evening. It started with a simple attempt to plan the weekend, but by now they had covered everything from the budget to his old girlfriends and her housekeeping . . . then on to the in-laws and whose fault it was that Justin was doing poorly in school. . . . The strangest part was that neither of them had any idea why their conversations always got so tangled.

No matter how long they talked, no matter how much they both wanted the downward spiral to stop, nothing changed. It had been this way for years. The only real change was in how long it took them to give up and go to their separate corners. After fifteen years they were both so weary of the process that they threw in the towel a little sooner. In the early years, arguments had frequently lasted for days.

99

At times I think the most difficult issue in marriage counseling is keeping two people on the same subject. It has been fascinating to sit in the counselor's chair and watch couples shift from subject to subject while solving nothing. I have often shaken my head in amazement and wondered, *If they communicate like this when they're in my office, what must it be like to live in their home?* If the scene were not so sad (and loud), it would be almost like a dance.

The dance goes something like this: A and B have been married for ten years. They are in my office and have stated on the forms that the central issue troubling them is their continual fighting over money. I say something intelligent like, "Tell me about that." And B begins to explain. The subject stays on the budget for maybe five sentences, when partner A makes a good point. Does this logic provide a step forward toward problem resolution? Not on your life!

When partner A makes a point, partner B's position is threatened. What if B can't get what she wants? What if A wins? Feeling weakened, partner B will avoid responding to the point but will instead deflect the attention of partner A by throwing out a verbal baited hook. Experience has taught partner B that partner A can't resist this particular subject, remark, or jibe. She knows A will chase the words like an old hound dog chases a fat squirrel crossing the path.

Suddenly the subject is no longer the budget but the fact that partner A lost fifty dollars last week on the office football pool. What would the pastor say if he knew his newest deacon was a gambler? Of course, now partner A is the one in a weakened position. Will he admit the error and go back to discussing the budget? Probably not. Instead, he fishes for a change of subject with his own baited hook: the amount lost was only half as much as partner B spent on new slacks and a blouse because partner B is twice the woman partner A married ten years ago!

By this point, the budget topic is totally abandoned. Embarrassment, wounded pride, guilt, charges of poor character, and the really big issues of life will trump dry discussions of the budget any day. The dance continues moving from subject to subject until the couple's mutual attacks become so painful, they call it quits with nothing resolved.

Of course, the dance of shifting subjects is not one exclusively reserved for Eeyores. We all do it. No one had to teach us how to avoid unpleasant realities by changing the subject. The skill is instinctual. Children learn it as soon as they learn to talk. But I think Eeyores do the dance especially well because centering on the negative aspects of life and relationship has given them plenty of ways to bait the hook!

In fairness, I should report that people of all levels of intelligence have a talent for hook baiting. I guess if we want a world where conversations are rational and stay on the subject until a solution is reached, we all need to possess a sweet nature, be a little dull mentally, and never have the desire to defend ourselves! Or it could work if we each were mature in Christ and willing to address our flaws rather than fight to cover them up.

Getting beyond our personal blocks and those of Eeyore is a challenge you won't always win. However, learning a few principles about communication will greatly increase your chance of getting your message through in spite of the static on the line.

In the previous chapter we looked at the skill of listening. Listening is major. You have earned the right to talk only after the other person feels that you have listened, really listened. But listening alone is not relationship. To connect with another, we must also learn to talk. Hopefully, this will be talk that takes one subject at a time and, as much as possible, is willing to avoid secondary gains.

Talk, Talk, Talk!

There are all types and levels of talking. Communication specialists have analyzed, categorized, and studied the spoken word backward, forward, and inside out. Many of their conclusions are enlightening, and some have actually been of practical help.

But the insights that have helped me most have seldom come from research analysis. What has taught me most about communicating with Eeyore (or anyone else) is simply doing it. At times I think I have made every communication blunder known to man. While practice has not made me perfect, it certainly has improved the final product!

I want to offer three truths about communication that have helped me tremendously. These are not techniques or even examples of how to do things. Rather, they are attitudes about what to expect from good communication. When my attitudes and expectations improved, then the practical give-and-take of healthy talking seemed to follow naturally.

Truth #1: Small Talk Ain't Small Potatoes

I have always been a what's-your-point, cut-to-the-chase kind of gal. What most people call small talk seemed like a royal waste of time to me. Patiently listening as others jumped through the hoops of social niceties or chatted about daily events never appealed to me. Unfortunately, much of that characteristic could also be described as pride, but I liked that word even less than I liked listening to small talk.

My spiritual maturity and communication skills took a huge step forward when I admitted that the God I worship is profoundly involved in huge amounts of detail. Much of what God created and cares for will never amount to anything. At least, it looks that way at times.

I live in a rural community. Around here, almost everyone gardens—and I don't mean a few roses. Our gardens are often extensive spaces of ground that feed the neighbors as well as the one working the hoe. It is nothing unusual to show up at church and have bags of tomatoes or cabbages sitting in the vestibule and the pastor giving a "Take whatever you want" invitation after the closing prayer.

When I came here as a bride from the city, the truth about gardening that amazed me most (besides the amount of work!) was the amount of waste involved in even a small plot of vegetables. There is far more trash than food. Only a small portion of most plants is edible, and even this portion varies greatly in size and quality. Much produce is thrown out. This seemed especially true of potatoes.

A potato bursts through the ground and makes a large, bushy plant. When the top blooms, the earth beneath it is turned over and the roots exposed. All along the spindly maze of thin roots are fleshy tubers. Potatoes. In our local soil, less than half of the potatoes will be large enough to eat; the rest range from pea size to the size of a quarter. The tiny ones are trashed. They are not worth the trouble of being picked up and cleaned. Maybe that is where the phrase "nothin' but small potatoes" originated.

Small talk is often thought of as "small potatoes"—something that incidentally occurs alongside "real" communication but is worthless for all practical purposes.

This is not true. The God who created small potatoes is interested in small things, even those things that on the surface appear to be useless. In nature, all that "trash" and "unimportant residue" produced by growing things falls back to the earth and creates a life-giving source for the next generation of produce. Without the trash there would be no harvest. Here is a demonstration of that concept, via a very important conversation:

Charlie came home from work tired and drained by the summer heat. He sincerely hoped that one day soon they could afford a car with a working air conditioner! He found Jeani in a hot kitchen canning jelly at the stove.

"Hi, hon," he said.

"Hi."

"Long day?"

"Yep," she answered while screwing tops on a dozen recently filled jars. "And you?"

"Yeah. Same old stuff. I'm gonna get a shower."

That brief exchange may not sound important, but it is. Any salesman knows that simple statements like "How are you?" and "Have a good day" make a difference in the amount of cash that will be in the drawer at the end of the day. Psychologist James Dobson, among others, states that the tone of the greetings during the first five minutes that people are together will set the mood of the household for the next several hours. The common, American interaction of "How are you?" "OK I guess. How about you?" is not a worthless greeting. It has monetary value to the salesman and emotional capital for the young married couple preparing to share an evening together.

Small talk is like grease on the gears of social interaction. It may not be the main attraction, but it smooths the process and enables deeper levels of connection to happen naturally at a later time.

Talking about the weather, the local ball team, and a new recipe for bean dip is not easy for many people—and it can be especially difficult for an Eeyore. He may be so problem-focused that everyday chatter seems useless or even offensive. That should not be used as an excuse to retreat into your personal shell and avoid him. It simply means that you and Eeyore both need more practice.

Remembering to greet someone and ask about his day does not always come naturally, but failure to do so can create unnecessary tension and an atmosphere that says you don't care about the other person. Small talk and social niceties are primary ways we respect each other. You can be an example of good communication to your Eeyore by regularly engaging in small talk.

A major characteristic of small talk is that it's positive in nature. Eeyore's cloud draws him to see the negative. Small talk pulls toward the positive. Expect to feel that tension when you chat with Eeyore. You don't have to pretend to be Pollyanna or never acknowledge life's difficult times, but try not to camp on problems for the night. Keeping a conversation with Eeyore on a positive plane is never easy. It would be a good idea to memorize and frequently review the instruction of Philippians 4:8: "Whatever is true, whatever is noble, whatever is right, whatever is pure, whatever is lovely, whatever is admirable—if anything is excellent or praiseworthy—think about such things" (*NIV*). When engaged in positive small talk with Eeyore, you are going to need all the encouragement you can get.

Truth #2: Getting to Know You Requires Sharing Emotion As Well As Information

Proverbs 18:21 assures us that "death and life are in the power of the tongue." God created the universe with his words (see Genesis 1). A lack of words creates pain. In Psalm 142 David cried in anguish because of his enemies. Part of his pain appears to be the isolation he felt. Various translations of verse 4 read that no one was there to "acknowledge" him, "regard" him, or "be concerned for" him. The result of the silence was a feeling that "no one cares for my soul."

Small talk is safe. Once we learn to do it well, we can engage in the process for hours and leave without knowing any more about the other person than when we started. It can also become a wall behind which we hide, keeping others at a safe distance. Some of us get stuck at the small-talk level and resist moving beyond it. It is possible to use words—even a good many of them—while still remaining isolated and giving others the impression that you don't "care for their souls." Small talk is good and very necessary, but really getting to know another person requires more.

Going beyond small talk compels us to add to our comfortable chatter those words that possess significance. I suspect that small talk makes up the bulk of our conversations—and it should—but far more relational capital is gained in the times when we share our hearts. That's when powerful words let another person know we truly care.

All talk is powerful stuff. Sharing information about ourselves is vital. But sharing our feelings kicks talking up to a whole new level. It is a level of vulnerability that many find uncomfortable. After small talk has laid the foundation, talking about feelings builds the home where we take our shoes off and share life comfortably with others.

Practicing this kind of talk is not too difficult. The simplest way is to make an effort to start some of our sentences with the phrase "I feel . . ."

Years ago I worked for a hospital psych unit. It was my job to lead group therapy, and five times a day I had to start the session by leading a "feelings round." Each participant, including the therapist, had to say "Hello, my name is _____, and I am feeling _____." As the leader, I had to set a good example and avoid trite words such as *tired* or *fine*. Talk about pressure! Being both honest and creative about my immediate feelings five times a day made me a walking thesaurus! The practice stretched my mind, heart, and vocabulary to the point where identifying personal feelings and putting them into words became second nature.

Words about feelings are where we let others touch

us and where we touch them. When we use words about feelings, we are on sacred ground. Talking about feelings is not as safe as talking about things and everyday events. Even the mention of emotion makes some people uncomfortable. But if we never get to the feeling level, Eeyore will remain an acquaintance and never be a companion. It is only at the feeling level that hearts begin to be shared.

However, I do need to add a word of caution. The old adage that everything should be done in moderation applies to talking about feelings as surely as it applies to the rest of life. Talking at a feeling level has its own particular pitfalls, and we need to be careful not to step in them.

One pitfall is when we believe that deep, intimate connections where soul touches soul are the only type of communication that is valuable. In the worst cases, individuals thrive on such conversations. Nothing else is seen as worthy. Every conversation needs to be about feelings—the deeper and more intimate, the better. Hardly a statement can be made that is not eagerly dissected for the feelings behind it. These individuals wear out themselves and everyone around them. Talking about our feelings is important, but like salt, a little goes a long way. Don't cheapen the treasure of soul-to-soul connection by insisting it stay around 24/7.

Truth #3: Silence Can Speak with Golden Words

All levels of communication flow through the channel of words. We must never devalue words, avoid them, or assume that another person "knows" even though we have never put our inner thoughts and feelings into words. However, communicating without words is also possible, and these wordless expressions can be pure gold.

We are surrounded by a constant stream of silent communication. Eyes, facial expressions, the way we hold our arms, and how we stand continually communicate to those around us. It all adds up to a small mountain of subtle messages being sent from one person to another. Within this mountain of physical expression, there are some physical touches that are never forgotten. These are rare moments full of tender emotion—times when soul touches soul and we know we are not alone. These times make us feel as if another person has stepped inside our skin and viewed our inner world with a peaceful acceptance. The person saw our most fragile memories and intimately knew secret hopes that we have scarcely breathed to ourselves . . . and then gathered it all in a tender embrace. No wonder such times are often called spiritual experiences; they are so much like what many people experience when they first touch Christ.

Death sometimes visits a family in waves. When I suddenly lost my husband, Bill, in 1979, my mother's husband, Jim, was in the last days of terminal lung cancer. Before the soil could settle on Bill's grave or Jim could draw his final breath, my mother's sister's husband was killed in a work accident.

These deaths were quickly followed by two more—my husband's brother and their mother.

I attended my uncle's funeral while still struggling through the depths of my own loss. Aunt Alma had requested a choir for her husband's funeral. As the last act of the service, the choir sang the "Hallelujah Chorus" while mourners filed out. I stood at the back of the room among the last to leave while Aunt Alma stood beside the coffin and raised her arms toward Heaven in a final salute to God in gratitude for her husband of fifty years.

The grief was overpowering as my mother slipped up behind me and put her arms around my shoulders. Her own grief was beyond words, knowing that her husband would soon join the ranks of the other men who had left our family. "God knows, God knows" was all she could say. It was enough.

Golden moments like these are both fragile and fleeting. The moments may be unutterably sad. They may be romantic. They may be expressed between generations, parent to child, or friend to friend. On very rare occasions they even occur between strangers drawn together by a mutual tragedy. These encounters cannot be orchestrated or forced to happen. If chased, they will vanish like a fist full of smoke we have grasped. But oh, how precious when they visit our lives.

As grand as golden moments are, real and living relationships are never grown from gold. Relationships thrive in the soil of the common, day-in-and-day-out interactions of two flawed humans seeking to cross the rivers that separate mankind. Relationship consists of the sparks and irritation found as iron sharpens iron (Proverbs 27:17). It encompasses the mistakes and frustrations and dedication to begin again. And if along the way you are surprised by a glimmer of gold, hold it with loose fingers and be grateful.

The Work of Talking

It is said that nothing worthwhile comes easily, and this is certainly true of good communication. The young couple in the park walking hand in hand may find it easy to talk for hours, but for the rest of us, talking can be just plain hard work. And given enough time, the young couple may find things change more quickly than they thought possible! Relaxing with small talk, connecting with feelings as well as facts, sending and receiving nonverbal messages, and allowing golden moments of soul-to-soul connection to come and fade in natural cycles constitute a huge task!

Complicating matters still more is the fact that the work of building relationship through good communication is seldom felt as an equal burden among partners. When Eeyore is trying to communicate with you, you may feel boxed in and overwhelmed by the negative flow. When you are trying to communicate with him, you may feel you are against an unresponsive brick wall. More than likely you will often feel as though you are doing the lion's share of the work while Eeyore gets a free ride!

But if we take the Bible seriously when it admonishes us to live peaceably with all whom God puts in our paths (Romans 12:18), communicating with even the most deeply morose Eeyore becomes not only possible but also necessary. One way the Bible urges us to fill that responsibility to live in peace is by learning to lay aside our own desires and adapt ourselves to filling the needs of others (Romans 15:1).

Personalities vary greatly in the number of words uttered each day. Some folks are natural chatterboxes, while others are comfortable with long stretches of silence. Adjustments on either end of the spectrum are necessary if we are to live in peace with another who is gifted differently. If our comfort with long silences makes another feel ignored, we should set our hearts to talk more. If our natural chattering overwhelms another, we must adjust these tendencies and talk less. Neither of these are easy assignments when our natures pull in the opposite direction.

This difficult situation would be easier if both partners were willing to bend, grow, and work. But too often one is willing while all the partner wants to do is drag his feet and complain. May your particular Eeyore be one who responds well and is grateful for your effort to create peace by adapting your natural communication style to fit his. If not, well, that is a different challenge. It is one that all your best efforts and reason, gratitude, listening, small talk, feelings-level communication, and patience can't be guaranteed to fix.

Eeyore can be a royal pain. His negative comments, withdrawal, and resistance to new ideas can torpedo a marriage, destroy a church, discourage a child, and generally make life miserable for everyone who must remain in relationship with him. There are times when he just needs a good, swift kick in the pants.

How to do that in a loving way is the subject of the next chapter.

> GET THE POINT

It takes thought, heart, and practice to communicate effectively.

>> READ THE BOOK

Examine Ecclesiastes 3:7; 5:2.

1. Much of the book of Ecclesiastes is advice about living a balanced life. For instance, sowing is balanced against reaping. In 3:7 what is talking balanced against? Do you know many people who have achieved the proper balance between these two things?

2. What further caution about words is added in 5:2?

Read Matthew 12:36; Psalm 19:14.

1. What importance did Jesus place on "idle words"?

2. What was David's prayer concerning the words of his mouth?

Look up Revelation 3:17, 18.

1. What example did Jesus give about people who were unaware of their true motives and real condition?

2. Can someone be held accountable for unconscious realities?

>>> TELL THE TRUTH

1. Does small talk come easily for you? How do you respond to the small talk of others?

2. Have you ever been surprised when the Holy Spirit revealed an attitude or motive in you of which you were unaware? How did you respond?

◄━ • • • • • ━►

CHAPTER SIX

Challenging Eeyore

"Nobody tells me," said Eeyore. "Nobody keeps me Informed. I make it seventeen days come Friday since anybody spoke to me."

"It certainly isn't seventeen days——"

"Come Friday," explained Eeyore.

"And today's Saturday," said Rabbit. "So that would make it eleven days. And I was here myself a week ago."

"Not conversing," said Eeyore. "Not first one and then the other. You said 'Hallo' and Flashed Past. I saw your tail in the distance as I was meditating my reply."

• • • • • • • • •

"It's your fault, Eeyore. You've never been to see any of us. You just stay here in this one corner of the Forest waiting for others to come to you. Why don't you go to them sometimes?"

There are times when every Eeyore needs a good, swift kick (metaphorically speaking, of course). I guess we all need that now and again. However, booting Eeyore with a word of correction can be a bit like kicking a porcupine. You take careful aim and do it quickly, but the end result is often pain for all concerned!

No doubt there is something about your Eeyore that drives you up a tree. The problem may be a little, irritating habit that has become like a dripping faucet on your last nerve. Or maybe the situation involves something serious that must be changed before your relationship with Eeyore can go on. Finding out how to approach this problem may be the very reason you're reading this book. If so, read carefully. The following may be the directions for which you have been waiting.

Confronting anyone about the error of his ways is extremely difficult. When dealing with Eeyore, the task borders on impossible. How do you "attack" someone who is down and depressed without pushing him over the edge? How does one successfully encourage change in someone whose life is centered on problems about which nothing is ever done? When is a confrontation worth the risk of things going wrong?

These aren't easy questions to answer, and chances are you won't manage the confrontation perfectly, no matter how well you plan or how hard you try. However, thinking through some of the problems in advance can increase the odds that real change will occur; doing nothing almost certainly assures that the problem will get worse.

Finding a way to help readers think through the process of confrontation was a challenge. Like most other activities of life, there are many ways to do it wrong and, often, more than one way to do it right. But after much deliberation, it seemed that the best method to show the wrong was through examples. And the best way to show the right was by giving a list of self-examination questions. If you want to help Eyore change his ways, please consider these points before venturing across the minefield of whatever is bugging you.

Confrontation: Doing It Wrong

If you asked Shirley, she would tell you that she always gives in and that the family never, ever considers her needs. But the truth is that for seventeen years she has ruled her family with a fist of iron. Everyone jumps when Shirley sighs. Everyone tries to cheer her when she mopes. Everyone gives Shirley what she wants when she cries.

The bandleader for this roll-over-and-give-her-what-she-wants march is her husband, Ben. During their courtship and early marriage, he gave in because he loved her and wanted to please her. After the children came along, he was terrified that if he stood against her demands, she would leave him and take his children.

Shirley's fear-based behavior smothered him, so he gradually became passive-aggressive. On the surface he said "yes, honey" to any given demand, but he manipulated in private to make sure it never happened. The kids followed his example, and by the time they reached their early teens, the family was in real trouble. Everyone, particularly Dad, was afraid of Mom's disapproval, complaints, and tears. But at the same time, they manipulated in the background to get their own ways. The manipulation was frequently exposed, and this was all the evidence Shirley needed to prove that everyone was against her.

By the time they sought counseling, the passive-aggressive patterns were so deeply ingrained in the teens—and the manipulative self-pity so firmly entrenched in Shirley—that little could be done to break the cycle.

For confrontation to work successfully, you must recognize from the beginning that confronting may cost you something. You must face the situation and try not to finagle a secret passage around it. You need courage to face it head-on. Such courage is not an absence of fear, but a willingness to do and say what is necessary—even when fear churns your insides and makes your hands sweat.

There are two common fears that keep people from confronting:

- the fear of losing the relationship
- the fear of disapproval

These fears create a wife who "can't" confront her husband's drinking problem because he might leave. These fears manifest themselves in an adult son who "can't" confront his elderly father about his need for regular bathing and clean clothes because, inside, the son is still ten years old and trembles when his father yells.

When we cower and refuse to confront, we may have made an idol of the other person and be demonstrating that we fear human disapproval more than we fear disobeying God. Or we may have made an idol out of our comfort and would rather let the other person continue in sin than risk upsetting our nest. Either way, one thing is certain: confronting is not for cowards.

Another way confrontation can go wrong is when we wait too long before we say what needs to be said. Such delayed action can allow emotions to build until confrontation becomes explosive.

Pam and Mandy were sisters. Both had brown hair, but that was where the similarity ended. Pam was outgoing and energetic; Mandy was moody and pessimistic. Pam was older; Mandy was fifteen years her junior.

When their widowed mother was diagnosed with breast cancer, both girls agreed that they would do all they could to help, even if it came to nursing their mom 24/7 in her home.

It did.

As circumstances neared the end, the girls took shifts

staying at the home in which they grew up. With the help of hospice and a part-time nurse, their mother would be allowed to die in the home where she had lived for forty years.

Pam was glad about the decision she and her sister had made, but she was unprepared for the extreme pressure such an arrangement involved. The grief. The demands. The innumerable details. The constant work. It was almost more than she could bear. Adding to her burden was the shocking way Mandy behaved. Pam was always the one who had to organize and initiate while Mandy moaned and did no more than was directly requested. As the workload became heavier and Pam's grief deepened, her anger toward her sister grew in proportion.

The final insult came the day Pam arrived for her shift and found two medications had completely run out while Mandy had been on duty. Mandy had not even called the pharmacy, much less picked up the needed prescriptions. Pam exploded.

She cried and yelled and told her sister the details of every resentment she had against her from childhood to the present. Her anger drove her to paint each complaint in terms of Mandy's poor character. Mandy cried and yelled back. Then, like a child, Mandy ran to her sick mother for comfort.

Pam's confrontation of her sister went badly because she delayed acting in a timely manner. She ended up in a situation where emotions, not truth and kindness, were ruling what came out of her mouth. It is probably impossible to keep emotions totally out of the confrontation process.

After all, if we weren't upset, confrontation would likely not be necessary in the first place. But when we delay matters until emotions become a driving force, we can almost be assured that our yelling and stomping will bring much heat and anger but little change.

Two major principles for successful confrontation are:

- Confront early before emotions take the lead.
- Always be prepared to stay on subject by being able to express specifically in three sentences or less what you want to see changed. (Note: This three-sentence how-to is spelled out on pages 137, 138 in the "Choosing Golden Words" section.)

There are probably more ways for confrontation to go wrong than can be covered in this brief space. But we'll deal with a couple more. One error that is more common than one might think occurs when we try to change things vicariously. We want the changes so desperately that we take on Eeyore's responsibility for him.

At the insistence of the school counselor, Samantha called my office and set up an appointment for her twelve-year-old daughter, Ashley. Minutes after the session began, Samantha was in tears.

She insisted that she had tried everything to keep her daughter out of trouble and there was nothing left she could possibly do. She selected clothes that were within the school dress code, but Ashley used her own money to buy that midriff-exposing, knit top that wrapped around her budding figure like spray paint.

As for homework, Samantha stayed up every night helping Ashley look up information, write reports, and work math problems. The teachers demanded too much. That was the problem. Ashley was a delicate child and often appeared sad. The school needed to "back off."

When I asked why Samantha had come to counseling alone when the appointment was for her daughter, she explained that she was there on Ashley's behalf. The appointment conflicted with a previously scheduled soccer game. Samantha explained, "I thought maybe you could just tell me what she needs to hear, and then I could talk to her about it after the game and tell her what you said."

"Let's see if I understand this correctly," I said with all the professionalism I could muster at the moment. "You have come to counseling as a substitute for your daughter because she is otherwise occupied." What amazed me most was that the mother agreed with this assessment and saw no problem with the arrangement.

The work of change is the exclusive responsibility of Eeyore and the Holy Spirit. You may advise. You may request. You may warn. You may hurt and cry. But no matter how much you want it, changing him is outside your power.

Some of the best advice I ever received about counseling came to me years ago from the pastor who directed our ministry at the Center for Christian Care. After I barged into his office, animatedly explaining my frustrating situation, he got a quizzical look on his face and peered over the top of his glasses, saying, "Elizabeth, something is wrong if you are working harder on this than your client seems to be."

Always remember that you can't change *for* Eeyore.

There is a balance needed when we undertake correcting another. Yet, like most things in life, confrontation can be overdone. As Adam's children, it is so easy for us to take the power of confrontation in our hands and twist it for our own selfish ends.

When Nesha's physician put her on medication for depression, she also recommended a life-management class offered by the local junior college. At first, Nesha was reluctant, but with the encouragement of her family, she decided to go. Although the family would later regret that decision, Nesha thought the experience delightful beyond measure. The instructor was young and very self-confident. She talked in terms of victims and survivors. She accented Nesha's rights, power, and autonomy.

It all made perfect sense once Nesha looked at life through the lens provided by the class. Her depression was not her fault. It was rooted in the fact that people ran over her. She was a victim; she needed to become a survivor.

Nesha gathered her courage and began confronting those around her.

Had her daughter left a dish in the living room and expected Mom to pick it up? Confront! Go on strike and refuse to clean house until the family shaped up and did their parts. Had her husband ignored her and spent too much time in front of the TV? Confront! Insist that he take her dancing or she would go by herself and have a great time without him. Had the church choir director unfairly awarded the Easter musical solo to another when Nesha was equally capable of hitting the high notes—and more faithful than most to attend rehearsals? Confront! She could find another church if this one did not treat her right.

From the time we are born, we humans seek our comfort and want our own ways. I don't think that is entirely a bad thing. Having specific desires and reaching for comfort are powerful motivators for progress. However, when our personal desires and comforts become the ultimate goal, and everyone—occasionally even God—is expected to gratify them, real trouble is at the door.

Confrontation is never to be used on a whim. It is not a tool to force the rest of the world into our way of thinking, and it is not a stick we use to beat others. We should never use confrontation as a weapon designed for selfish ends.

Before you march forth to confront Eeyore, it would be a good idea to review the five principles mentioned in this section:

1. Confronting is not for cowards.

2. If you must confront, do it early before emotions take the lead.

3. Never attempt confrontation until you can write out your request in three sentences or less.

4. Remember that Eeyore must do the work.

5. Never let confrontation become a tool to achieve selfish ends.

Confrontation: Doing It Right

If Eeyore is getting on your nerves and you feel yourself about to blow, it's time to confront the situation. If Eeyore is destroying his life or yours, it is time to confront. Confrontation for a minor situation may look and feel substantially different than one in which life-changing issues are involved, but both share some basic processes and principles that are worth considering in advance.

These involve making sure your motives and approach are right. And the best way I know to do that is to prayerfully work your way through a list of specific questions. Like a pilot going over a preflight checklist, going over these questions may save you a major crash.

The following questions are carefully crafted to help you avoid common pitfalls. They are specific and center on Eeyore's *behavior*—not his character or his feelings— and they clarify your own motives for acting. Challenging

Eeyore's character often leads to endless debates that are better left to the Holy Spirit. Challenging his feelings is a sure no-win situation, for you can't prove what you only suspect. But centering the confrontation on Eeyore's behaviors and *your* personal feelings is safe. Behaviors are observable and provable, and no one but you can say what you feel inside.

Take your time. Pray about it. And as you consider telling Eeyore what he needs to change, ask yourself the following:

Q. Is Eeyore's behavior against God's laws?

The first action Eeyore (or anyone else) often takes when confronted with a need to change is to attack the messenger. You may be accused of pride or self-interest or told that you have no right to judge. Prepare for that likelihood in advance. If you have thought it through and know beyond doubt that the behavior is against God's law, you may be better prepared to deflect a few of the arrows that come your way. Eeyore's accusations may hurt, but you have assurance that you are not to blame. You didn't make the rules; God did. If Eeyore has an argument with God's rules, tell him to take it to the Boss.

Inappropriate behaviors against God's law may include the obvious biggies such as adultery or drunkenness, but they are not limited to that. An adolescent Eeyore who constantly grumbles, grouses, and complains can be reminded that it's serious—God at one time killed folks for that (see Numbers 11:1-3). Or there may be a situation in which to point out that we have been instructed by God to "do everything without complaining" (Philippians 2:14, *NIV*).

Just remember that using God's laws to give correction can backfire. After all, when God gave a rule to Eeyore, he did not exempt Piglet.

Q. Will the behavior physically damage anyone?

To answer this question, make sure your definition of *damage* is broad enough. Don't limit the concept to bloodletting. An elderly parent who often leaves the burner on under a pot is physically dangerous to himself and possibly others. A father who drinks and drives is physically dangerous to the children he has in the car as well as to other motorists on the road.

Q. Is this behavior damaging to character?

Sometimes Eeyore's behavior may be hard to pin down to a certain Bible verse or biblical principle. An example is a young mother who becomes so engrossed in Christian romance novels that her heart is slowly changed toward her real—and faulty—husband. There is nothing wrong or unscriptural about reading a clean romance novel. But when character and faith begin to be eroded by any habit—food, friends, music, money—then it is time for those who care about Eeyore to confront him and request that he examine these things in the light of eternal values.

But these slow-change, character-threatening problems are the most difficult to challenge. Character matters, but when you say "I see your heart is not with the Lord as it used to be," Eeyore can just as quickly counter with "That's not true." Unless you have solid examples of behavioral change, you will lose the confrontation before you begin. If it is an issue of character that needs to change, find a way to put it in behavioral examples. Otherwise, keep your suspicions to yourself.

Q. Is the behavior not sinful but simply something I want?

There is nothing wrong with confronting someone simply because a change in his behavior is important to you. If Eeyore snores to the extent that the noise is keeping you up at night, and you know a simple nose clamp would help the situation, but Eeyore refuses to wear one, confront! A behavior does not have to be sinful, illegal, or full of character assassination to be worthy of discussion. Our personal preferences, comfort, and even curious notions are worth consideration.

Confrontation at this level has a very different tenor than the life-change variety, but it is still important and appropriate. Make your desires known, but also allow plenty of room for alternate suggestions and consideration of Eeyore's preferences.

Q. If I were in his place, would I want someone to correct me?

This question (based on the Golden Rule of Matthew 7:12) is the watershed issue for all confrontation. Above all else it will guide your decision about how to confront—and indeed whether confrontation is wise and necessary. When asked with an honest heart, this question will almost never fail to lead you in the right direction.

Rightly asked, the question also has other rewards. Even if Eeyore never changes his behavior, you will have peace knowing that you did the right thing. You will also have shown courage by doing your best to put love into practice. Heaven notices such things.

Q. Will my confrontation have a chance of success?

Of course there is a chance of success. A very good one. Well-planned and lovingly delivered words of correction are vital and often used by God to turn another person around.

However, there are no guarantees that even the most needed, carefully planned, and lovingly delivered confrontation will always be successful. Do everything right, and things can still go wrong. But we can greatly reduce that risk if we will honestly evaluate our situation in advance and eliminate those situations for which the chance of success is almost certainly zero. In situations like that, you probably should not attempt confrontation in the first place; it would only be casting your pearls before swine (see Matthew 7:6).

Here are two common examples of situations with a near-zero success rate:

- those relationships that are already so knotted and strained that everyday conversations create anger
- situations where Eeyore has crossed the thin line of rationality and no longer responds to logical argument or evidence

Brenda's mother called her five to eight times a day, every day. She complained and moaned and picked apart every comment Brenda made. Brenda had tried to get her mother interested in other things and had often told her she was too busy to spend hours on the phone. Mom ignored all suggestions and became insulted at the very idea that Brenda might not want to talk to her mother. In this case, it would probably be useless for Brenda to confront her mother. A better solution would be an answering machine and caller ID.

The Necessity of Confrontation

After you have thought about all the ways confrontation could go wrong and have asked yourself all the pertinent questions and recognized the risk involved, you may begin to think that confrontation is simply not worth it. Wrong.

Confrontation is necessary. It is even inescapable. Despite all the difficulty and risk, it is one of the basic dynamics of life that we cannot—and should not—avoid.

If we do not stand up for what is right, evil takes over. If we neglect our responsibility to correct the dependents God has placed in our paths (students, children, aging parents), we will pay for our negligence in this world as well as the next. Ezekiel 33:7-9 seems to bear this out. If we don't stand up for our own rights, we may be guilty of sin because we have willingly allowed another to sin against us and have thereby participated in his evil! (also see 1 Timothy 5:22). If we do not help others sharpen their characters, our lack of passion leaves them to struggle alone and makes room for Satan's attack. If we are so fearful of disapproval or the loss of relationship that we refuse to challenge another when it is needed, we are guilty of elevating that person to the position of being an idol. We must fear no one but God alone.

The list could go on. But the bottom line is that for us to be what God calls us to be, we must be willing to confront. If we love our Eeyore and want to act as a friend, appropriate confrontation is a must.

King Solomon was reportedly the wisest man who ever lived. But if you follow his story, it is evident that he was far better at giving wise advice than bringing his personal behavior into line. Maybe his story would have been different if he'd had an honest friend like the one who corrected his father, David. The account of David's sin with Bathsheba, followed by Nathan's rebuke, is found in 2 Samuel 11, 12.

Even though Solomon drifted from God's ways and seems never to have corrected much of his own behavior, he was wise enough to see the value of having a friend with enough courage to communicate hard truths. He wrote in Proverbs 27:6, "Faithful are the wounds of a friend." A true friend will occasionally deliver a wound if doing so will put you back on the right track. A friend will not be so fearful of your disapproval that he says nothing and lets you walk off a cliff.

The real question usually is not *whether* we should confront another but *how* we should do it. Happily, God did not leave us twisting in the wind, but gave clear directions in several Bible passages:

- "If your brother sins against you, go and tell him his fault between you and him alone. If he hears you, you have gained your brother. But if he will not hear you, take with you one or two more, that 'by the mouth of two or three witnesses every word may be established.' And if he refuses to hear them, tell it to the church. But if he refuses even to hear the church, let him be to you like a heathen" (Matthew 18:15-17).

- "Speaking the truth in love, [you] may grow up in all things into Him who is the head—Christ" (Ephesians 4:15).
- "Let the word of Christ dwell in you richly in all wisdom, teaching and admonishing one another in psalms and hymns and spiritual songs, singing with grace in your hearts to the Lord" (Colossians 3:16).
- "All Scripture is given by inspiration of God, and is profitable for doctrine, for reproof, for correction, for instruction in righteousness" (2 Timothy 3:16).

One of the most comprehensive statements about communication and confrontation is given to us in Proverbs 25:11: "A word aptly spoken is like apples of gold in settings of silver" (*NIV*). This is another of those jewels left to us by Solomon. The statement is simple and brief, but it holds enough power to keep any confrontation on track and assures the best results possible. We are to choose words that are apt and place them in the proper settings. An apt word is one that is fitting, proper, suitable, and right. And the proper setting involves situation, scenery, and surroundings.

Choosing Golden Words

The first step in successful confrontation is to determine *exactly* what you want to say. That should be a no-brainer.

136

Unfortunately, when it comes to confrontation, humans often lead with their emotions while the brain is relegated to the position of caboose.

This unfortunate leading-with-the-heart approach usually results in a discussion that disintegrates into what I refer to as a moving-target argument. As mentioned before, putting someone on the defensive by changing the subject is a favored way of defending ourselves and avoiding personal change. When Joe tells Mary that she shouldn't spend so much money eating out, Mary can avoid a discussion of the issue by diverting the subject to Joe's reluctance to ask his boss for a raise.

When preparing to confront, you should be able to put your request in no more than three sentences. The fewer words you have to remember while under fire, the more likely you will be able to stay on the central issue. I very much encourage writing out these sentences. Don't want to write? Then at least rehearse the golden words in your mind until you can say them in your sleep.

- *Sentence one.* A good pattern is to assure the person of your love and loyalty: "Mary, I know how hard it is for you to teach all day and then come home to the demands of a house and hungry family."
- *Sentence two.* State exactly what the problem is: "However, I kept track last week, and if we continue in this way, we will have spent three

thousand dollars on restaurant food by the end of the year."

- *Sentence three.* State exactly what changes you want to see made: "If we could agree to eat at home during the week, we could hire a babysitter and go out twice a month."

I deliberately chose a simple situation for the purpose of example, but you get the idea. Be direct, be specific, and clearly give your suggestion for change. And while you are at it, there are two other good rules to remember:

- When possible, use "I feel" statements rather than ones that begin with "You should."
- Put your request in the context of behavior rather than bad character.

People do possess bad character and rotten attitudes, but it is best to avoid mentioning these during a confrontation. In the three-sentence example for Joe and Mary, you will note that Joe could have used words like *selfish, lazy, spendthrift,* and *stupid,* but he didn't. He remained on target, identifying a behavior he had observed and stating why that behavior needed to change.

Sometimes a fourth sentence needs to be added to a statement of confrontation. This sentence is not about Eeyore. It's about you. Sometimes it is necessary to tell

Eeyore exactly what you intend to do if he or she refuses to change. This part of confrontation requires the most forethought and courage. It is not a time for empty threats or emotional outbursts. This sentence reads: "If you don't _____, then I will _____."

Unfortunately, thinking ahead about this fourth step is often lacking when serious confrontations are underway. People end up saying impromptu—and dumb—things like:

- "If you don't bring up your grades, I'll ground you for the next six months." (*Highly unlikely to be enforced.*)
- "If you don't quit drinking, I'll die." (*No, you won't.*)
- "If you don't start helping out more around the house, I'll beat you to within an inch of your life." (*Illegal.*)
- "If you don't stick to the budget, I'll go out and buy that new car I've been wanting." (*Stupid.*)
- "If you won't lose weight on your own, I'll make you." (*Impossible.*)

There are many times when closing a confrontation with a warning about your future intent is appropriate and even necessary. But, by all means, think about what you are saying. Choose realistic options you have the power and willingness to carry out, and never threaten something you are unwilling or unable to do.

In most cases there are actions that you can choose over which Eeyore has no control. These options may inconvenience or even hurt you, but they may be necessary all the same. (This is especially true if you are confronting Eeyore about a behavior that is life threatening.) A couple examples of options are: sending a teen to live with his natural father if he refuses to quit skipping school; or separating from a mate who refuses to face his drug addiction.

The centerpiece of confrontation is the choosing (and rehearsal) of appropriate words. Once they have been chosen, then it is time to find the proper setting in which to place them.

Framing the Words in Silver

Before someone can listen, you must have his attention. When you want Eeyore's attention, you will probably have to capture it on the fly. His attention floats from one flaw/problem/danger to the next with little time lapse in between. So if you want him to listen, you need to choose a time when, and a setting where, as much as possible is "right" with his world. Otherwise, your message will be lost. His preoccupation with the next difficulty on the list will derail the issue and get you off subject before you even begin. So we come to the "settings of silver" part of Proverbs 25:11.

How will you find an opportune moment? I know,

your Eeyore is constantly generating his own dark clouds. Nonstop. But still, there will be times and seasons when he is more open to conversation and less distracted by things that need fixing.

You have had time to observe your Eeyore. What are the places, times of day, and conditions when he is least distracted by problems?

It would be a bad idea for someone to approach me in the morning. I don't do mornings. I even suggest this characteristic is pietistic. After all, Lucifer is called "son of the morning" (Isaiah 14:12), and I wouldn't want to be like him! Others believe that God created the morning specifically to rejuvenate them personally, and they feel lost all day if they don't see the sunrise. Amazing. Another bad time for me is right after I finish my work day. I need time to reorient without being pressured for conversation or answers. I figure there will be enough time for conversation and answers later . . . after my nap.

Your Eeyore has biorhythms; he has locations where he feels most secure. Use these to your advantage. God approves. Honest. If you want Eeyore to hear something important, make sure you find a highly polished "setting of silver" to encase the message.

Meeting at a restaurant may be a good choice. Most folks are more receptive when their bellies are full. There are still a few restaurants with somewhat pleasant music and without the racket of a TV. Find one.

It may be that your particular Eeyore is most receptive in his own home. Eeyore may live with you or across town, but wherever home is, it could become a pleasant setting for your golden words.

Whatever the setting, it is a good idea to have your own transportation close by. This is especially important if you are confronting a really big or emotionally charged issue. People often need time to work through the emotion of your challenge. Allow that time with grace. Never let the confrontation drag on for an extended time; the risk of slipping off the issue is too great. Keep going back to your golden words that have been memorized and rehearsed. Stick with those words until you either get an answer or a commitment of when an answer will be given. If no progress at all is being made, suggest that the matter be taken up again at another time, and exit.

The time of day and physical setting are important. But there are other, more subtle, aspects that add luster to your setting of silver. One of the most influential of these is your personal mood. It is easy to confront someone when your anger is hot and the situation desperate. It is quite another thing to coolly think through what needs to be said, figure out the time and place to say it, and then deliver the message with a loving attitude. Three things that help assure your cool, calculated approach are time, rehearsal, and prayer.

Time. Choose the time; don't let the time choose you. Never confront when the situation is right on top of you.

Wait until later when the storm has passed and shifting emotions are not driving you. If you have to, literally bite your tongue and physically move away from the situation. When emotions are in the driver's seat, there is little room for the brain to take the wheel.

Rehearsal. Rehearse what you need to say. Then edit, minimize, and rehearse again. Every time you think through the words and imagine possible outcomes, you reduce the emotional charge the situation carries. The less driven by emotion you can become, the less likely Eeyore will be able to use your emotional state as an excuse for not dealing with your challenge.

Prayer. Through it all, your most powerful weapon for keeping your cool is prayer, both your personal prayer and that of like-minded individuals who are willing to be a spiritual support. "More things are wrought by prayer than this world dreams of"[3] is a classic saying that still applies today. God hasn't changed. He can still take an old donkey and turn him completely around.

Above all, your setting of silver should glow with the polish of genuine love. We are specifically told in Ephesians 4:15 that love is a prerequisite when we have to speak words of correction. Start off by stating your love. Be prepared to give an example of your loving actions from the past. Love always seeks the best for the beloved, so share with Eeyore why you believe a positive response to your challenge will improve his life. Close with a reassurance of your love.

You may not be able to convince Eeyore that your challenge is coming from a heart of love and is intended for his good, but you will have a clear conscience knowing that out of right motives you did your best. That knowledge is priceless—especially if the results are not what you desired and the whole situation goes south.

Who's in Charge Here?

Perhaps the most frightening thing about challenging Eeyore (or anyone else) is that the outcome cannot be assured in advance. No matter how much the word of correction may be needed, no matter how carefully you lay the foundation, no matter how much you pray and hope, the end results are up to Eeyore, not you. This goes back to what was said earlier: You can't learn, behave, think, or feel for someone else. Eeyore must do the work of change.

When Eeyore refuses to do the work of change, there may come extreme situations when you must exert physical and/or legal authority. But even in those situations, you are still not in total control. You may find there is a time you can force Eeyore's body, but you will never be able to choose his feelings, behavior, and beliefs for him.

Feelings. You can physically hang on to a nine-year-old and make him go to the doctor for a shot, but you can't make him happy about the situation.

Behavior. You can send a rebellious teenager to live with his uncle in Mississippi, but you can't stop him from hitchhiking back to California to see his girlfriend.

Beliefs. You can get a court order through Adult Protective Services, giving you control of an aging parent's bank account, but you can't make him believe that you have taken the action because you love him.

Confrontation is a process inherently fraught with pitfalls, problems, and unpredictable outcomes. But no matter how out of control the situation may seem, always remember that it is never beyond the control of God. When you have answered the pertinent questions and know in your heart that your desire is to do good—not cause pain— you can rest. God has not abdicated his throne. Your only responsibility is to provide an opportunity for Eeyore to change. Whether or not change occurs is up to him. Final control is up to God.

> GET THE POINT

Christians have a responsibility to spur one another on to good deeds and better character development, and sometimes that involves a loving confrontation.

> > READ THE BOOK

Study Matthew 7:1, 2, 5; 1 Corinthians 6:1-5.

1. Some people have suggested that Matthew 7:1 is the most commonly quoted Scripture in the Bible. It is also one of the most misunderstood. Does the Bible say that we are not to judge one another? What do you think Jesus meant?

2. Compare the above Scriptures. What do you believe to be their central teaching concerning judging others?

Investigate Hebrews 10:24-27.

1. Verse 24 in the *KJV* says we are to "provoke" one another to love and good works, while the *NIV* uses the phrase "spur one another on." The *NKJV* says we are to "stir up." How would *you* express this concept?

2. Verses 26, 27 give the reason why we are to provoke, spur, and stir. What is it?

Read Proverbs 27:6.

1. What does this passage say about a real friend who causes pain? When is causing such pain appropriate?

2. Describe an incident when someone was hurt by words or actions that appeared on the surface to be kind.

➤ ➤ ➤ TELL THE TRUTH

1. Recall a time when someone successfully challenged you to change or a time when you successfully challenged someone else.

2. Do you consider yourself conflict-avoidant?

3. Why does God want us to learn to properly challenge each other?

>−·····−<

CHAPTER SEVEN

Eeyore's Friends

It was going to be one of Rabbit's busy days. As soon as he woke up he felt important, as if everything depended upon him. It was just the day for organizing Something, or for Writing a Notice Signed Rabbit, or for Seeing What Everybody Else Thought About It. It was a perfect morning for hurrying round to Pooh, and saying, "Very well, then, I'll tell Piglet," and then going to Piglet, and saying, "Pooh thinks—but perhaps I'd better see Owl first." It was a Captainish sort of day, when everybody said, "Yes, Rabbit" and "No, Rabbit," and waited until he had told them.

God has a sense of humor. If he didn't, he would have populated the planet with one-size-fits-all personalities. Everyone would think the same, behave the same, and laugh at all the same jokes. No one would be extroverted, introverted, quick-tempered, or shy. All people could be a nice, bland vanilla, rather than the tutti-frutti mix that now complicates our relationships.

But God didn't choose to do it that way. He took great care to form personalities in a kaleidoscope of brilliant hues. Like snowflakes, no two are exactly alike. The extensive variety must give him great pleasure, or he certainly went to a lot of trouble for nothing. And as Hamlet said, "There's the rub."

Our differences are the things that irritate, confuse, and enchant us. They make life interesting and at the same time painful, as one personality rakes against another and knocks off the rough edges. Differences force us to communicate in ways that are unfamiliar and uncomfortable. They make us stand amazed as we scratch our heads wondering why others can't understand us when we all speak the same language. Connecting with other personalities requires us to bend when we'd rather stiffen, and to stand when we would rather melt away. All in all, the situation is quite impossible. "Oh, bother," as Pooh would say.

The writings of Pooh creator A. A. Milne have enchanted adults as well as children for eighty years. One reason is the distinct way in which he honors God's great variety of personalities, while at the same time accenting those idiosyncrasies with which we best identify.

When reading *Winnie-the-Pooh* or *The House at Pooh Corner,* one is almost guaranteed to meet some relative, childhood friend, or coworker who is just like Tigger or Rabbit or Owl, not to mention Eeyore. Milne's insight into the interplay between these characters is keen. To have accomplished so much within the framework of a child's interest and vocabulary is truly phenomenal.

Yet isn't this exactly what we should expect from any creative writer? A good writer must be able to pick out particular mannerisms, words, and expressions that show distinctness of personhood. Characters are fleshed out with a unique set of details that distinguish them and make them breathe on paper. But if the distinctions are carried too far, the character will feel foreign to the audience and somehow fake. Every detail must be held in balance. The personality traits must all fit together to form a tapestry that is both distinct and vaguely familiar. The better a writer can do that, the more connected we feel to each character and the more easily we identify them with real people we know.

The fact that characters *do* resemble people we know assures us that for all the variety within God's creation, there is also a sameness, an order, allowing us to see people as groups as well as individuals. Identifying exactly which traits, mannerisms, feelings, and thinking patterns best represent a particular group has fascinated not only writers but also scientists for centuries.

Pigeonholing People

I am not sure where the term *pigeonhole* came from. Perhaps pigeons in cages have small cubbies where the birds make neat nests. But no matter the source, I like pigeonholes very much—especially when I am working. I always feel better when I can take a file, paper, stray pencil, or CD and put it in its proper place along a neat row of small boxes. Pigeonholes are a great asset.

Anything in several varieties becomes more manageable when similar items are grouped together, creating order. We sort everything from papers on a desk to trash for recycling. We also sort people. The process is unavoidable, and as long as we balance the sorting with a healthy respect for individual differences, it is not a bad thing. Scientists have been trying to pigeonhole people for thousands of years.

The Greek physician Hippocrates (460–377 BC) may have been the first social researcher. He looked around at the immense variety of fellow human beings and decided they could fit into four groups.[4] Not knowing much about brains at the time, Hippocrates thought individual personality developed from a balance of body fluids: black bile (melancholic temperament), yellow bile (choleric temperament), phlegm (phlegmatic temperament), and blood (sanguine temperament). According to Hippocrates, emotional stability depended on a balance of the four fluids; an excess of one fluid or the other produced physical illness or an exaggerated personality trait.

A person with too much black bile (dark blood perhaps mixed with other secretions) was believed to produce a melancholic (depressed) temperament. An oversupply of yellow bile (secreted by the liver) would result in anger, irritability, and a "jaundiced" view of life. An abundance of phlegm (secreted in the respiratory passages) was thought to make people stolid, apathetic, and undemonstrative. And, of course, bright red blood produced a bright and happy personality that was full of energy.

Hippocrates must have been on to something. The belief that personalities are rooted in physical realities is still a part of us today—though the belief that personality comes from body fluids has been replaced by the belief that it arises from synaptic gaps and neurotransmitters.

Hippocrates was also ahead of his time when he divided personalities into four categories. There have been hundreds of personality theories proposed since that time, and most of them utilize some combination of four categories. (A notable exception is an Enneagram based on a division of nine.)

In the late 1920s Isabelle Myers started working with the theories of C. G. Jung. She was fascinated with his division of personalities into two divisions, extroverts and introverts, but knew this designation alone was insufficient. Later, her daughter, Katharine Briggs, joined her in the careful and deeply researched work. By 1943 they were ready to publish the Myers-Briggs Personality Inventory. This highly popular test divides the human race into four continuums of basic characteristics: Extroverted/Introverted (E/I), Sensing/Intuition (S/N), Thinking/Feeling (T/F), and Judging/Perceiving (J/P). The system worked well and is widely in use today.

Thirty years ago, Tim LaHaye used a spin-off of Hippocrates' work when he wrote *Spirit-Controlled Temperament*. He even retained much of the ancient terminology. In the late 1980s, Gary Smalley and John Trent got together, and by 1990 they gave birth to *The Two Sides of Love*. Through them we learned that determining whether you were a beaver, lion, golden retriever, or otter was an important issue.

The secular community was not far behind; by the mid-1990s we were working with red, blue, yellow, and white personalities.[5] In Tennessee, T-shirts of appropriate colors were given out in the public schools, encouraging children each to know their own personality color and to honor the colors of others.

Almost all of us can remember a personality test we either took during a seminar, clipped from a magazine, filled in during a job interview, or received from a professional who told us what type personality we possessed and how we were likely to interact with others. As a professional in the field, I have taken more than my share of these, and as best I can figure, I am a choleric, blue beaver with a P/T/S who splits the E/I continuum almost exactly in half! Another dozen nomenclatures could be added, and most—but not all—would be based in some division of four.

With all these fours and animal-types crawling about, I suspect I will cover most of humankind rather thoroughly by discussing how Eeyore relates to four of his friends.

Eeyore and Rabbit

I identify with Rabbit more than with any of Milne's other characters. Rabbit always has an agenda and is never happier than when in control of some project. Rabbits and Eeyores will inevitably clash. While both will be better for the collision, each will be a bit addled by it as well.

Shawn rehearsed his list as he shaved. Even though it was Saturday, he wanted to stop by the office briefly and check on the new computer backup CDs. But he had also made a commitment to spend more time with the kids. A recent sermon had convicted him of lack in this area, and above all, he wanted to be a good father. Maybe he and Susan could have a date night. That would be good. Of course, the lawn also needed attention.

When he returned to the bedroom, Susan was still asleep. He gently shook her shoulder. "Hon, I am going to run by the office for a minute, but I'll be back in about an hour. Why don't you and the kids have breakfast, and then I'll take them to the park. Or better yet, maybe we could all go for a picnic lunch. Be back soon."

He was looking forward to a well-planned day, but when he returned home just before 10:00 AM, things were not at all as he expected. His three kids were munching a do-it-yourself breakfast of cereal and juice, and his wife was in the shower. Shawn opened the bathroom door and fought his way through a cloud of steam. "What about our picnic?" he shouted above the sound of rushing water

"I don't know," said his noncommitting wife. "We are out of bologna, and if I have to go to the store for that, I may as well buy groceries. But if I buy groceries, there won't be time to pack a lunch. We might not get to the park before one thirty. It will be awfully hot by that time of day."

Shawn was disgusted. Why couldn't that woman ever get on board with what he knew was best for the family? How could he fulfill his role as leader if she wouldn't follow? Susan is just rebellious and unwilling to do her part in God's plan, *he thought.*

Shawn didn't know it, but his evaluation of Susan was dead wrong. This was not a clash of wills or a situation of rebellion against leadership. Shawn-the-Rabbit was just having a normal conversation with Susan-the-Eeyore.

The thing that irritates Rabbits most when relating to Eeyores is their woeful, wishy-washy approach to life.

157

Because Eeyores see problems to the right, they pause. Then on further consideration, they see problems to the left. Another pause. Reconsideration has them thinking about further problems that would probably arise if they went straight ahead. Processing all that data takes time. In fact, it may take so much time that action stops altogether.

Rabbits who live with Eeyores have two choices: take charge or take a rest.

There are times when Rabbit needs to take charge and bulldoze right past Eeyore. Someone has to initiate action, and *action* is Rabbit's middle name. Eeyore's negativism, resistance, and fears could stagnate until the world stopped spinning. He needs someone—and, strangely, appreciates someone—who will move in and take over. Of course, when you move forward and make decisions, expect Eeyore to notice if things don't work out. Consider his "I told you so" to be a tax paid on the price of leadership, and let it go.

However, there are times when taking charge is the last thing a wise Rabbit should do. Good leaders look for occasions to stand back and give others room to process. It can be wise to let Eeyore taste the responsibility of leadership whether he wants it or not. If Rabbit is always taking charge, the only thing Eeyore will learn is resentment.

These two choices raise an interesting challenge for Rabbit. How does he know when to do which? Shall he move in and take charge or back off and let Eeyore process the problem?

The bad news is that for your specific situation, I don't have a clue. The good news is that the Holy Spirit knows exactly what you should do and is willing to share that information with any Rabbit willing to listen. You may have to humble yourself and admit your confusion. You may have to lay aside your personal agenda and listen to Eeyore's wisdom and justified criticisms. You may have to trust God's ability to control the situation even when you can't clearly hear his voice. But over time you will find that God has led and that his ways were best.

Eeyore and Piglet

Remember Piglet? The shy little creature with large, excited ears? He and Eeyore make an unusual pair. Eeyore's fears are largely of his own making, and he has a stubborn streak that resists even the possibility of good. Piglet, too, is fearful, but his fears are of a different quality. Timid and easily frightened, Piglet is also pliable and willing to try if the prize is tempting enough.

Jody felt the energy of the piano flow through her fingers as she went over the recital piece one more time. Had the slight tremor that plagued her earlier in the week passed? Were the notes still weak at the point where power was required? Maybe. Perhaps she should not have tried out for the scholarship.

Her mother entered the room softly and sat listening to

Jody play. So much depended on next Thursday's audition. She could imagine Jody's tears if the judges gave her low marks. The vision grieved her. Why had her precious daughter insisted on trying out? Yes, she had won the last four rounds of competition, but now she faced the best of the best. Her mother listened to the beautiful, complicated music and thought she heard a weakness in the upper notes. "Don't forget those high notes. They are really important." She hoped her correction would help.

The words stung. Jody continued to play, but her heart beat faster, and notes were less sure.

"I just wanted to remind you that it is really OK if you lose," said her mother. "Not everyone must go to college to be a success." She wanted desperately to ease the pain if Jody should lose. Preparing her in advance seemed a wise thing. Then if she won, it would be a pleasant surprise, not an expectation.

On the other side of the room, Jody experienced the words very differently than her mother intended. Even my own mother doesn't think I can win, the discouraging thought repeated over and over as the music rose to a crescendo. Jody-the-Piglet had just collided with Mama-the-Eeyore.

When Piglet relates to Eeyore, his major task is to resist being overwhelmed. That is not easy because almost everyone overwhelms Piglet.

Being overwhelmed by Tigger or Rabbit is not so bad for Piglet. He can join Tigger's excitement and follow Rabbit's plans, secure in the confidence of others. Even relating to Owl is not too difficult. All Piglet must do is avoid falling asleep amid the tons of Owl's analytical verbiage. But Eeyore challenges Piglet to the core. For the timid to be overwhelmed by those who resist hope is a tragic thing indeed.

Yet Piglet can learn some things from Eeyore better than from any other creature in the forest. Eeyore's warnings and negative meanderings push Piglet to courage. Eeyore gives voice to Piglet's own worst fears and makes him face possibilities that he would rather avoid.

The apostle Paul instructs us to "encourage the timid" (1 Thessalonians 5:14, *NIV*). One way to do that is by saying "You can make it. I know you will succeed," but another way is to force the timid to face the fear. This is a service Eeyore does best. When in close relationship with Eeyore, Piglet has to continually push himself to stand against Eeyore's dire predictions of failure. While nerve-racking, the technique is not ineffectual. The results can lead to Piglet's becoming a much stronger little pig.

Eeyore and Tigger

Perhaps no combination in the forest is so difficult and problem laden as that of Eeyore and Tigger. There are more misunderstandings, more obstructions, and more difficulties in this combination than any other. Tigger is all about parties and flash and sparkle. Tiggers move quickly and think later. These characteristics are diametrically opposed to everything in Eeyore's spirit.

Taking over the family-owned business seemed like a dream come true to Danny. When Grandfather Bishop started the appliance store in 1925, the very concept of a building with nothing in it but household machines was a novelty. But the dreams that others viewed skeptically became reality. Year by year, small expansion and successes built a lively income for Grandfather Bishop, his two sons, and later his grandsons. Danny's father took over the business in 1962 and ran the operation with equal success until his retirement last year.

At first, Dad's retirement created a small power struggle. Danny and his cousin Vance had both worked in the business since they were teens. Vance was older and more experienced. But in the end, Danny's enthusiasm and salesmanship won, and Vance became the company vice president. There were no hard feelings. The family was at peace—until the months dragged on and Danny found communicating with his slower, methodical, negative cousin an almost impossible challenge.

Danny was all about flash and sparkle. The first day in his new position, he made plans to repaint the showroom and expand the product line. He was less than pleased when Vance and the accountant showed him how the disruption and expense involved in these projects was likely to impact current sales.

As the weeks continued, those two kept teaming up to throw a wet blanket on Danny's dreams. Even when the accountant smiled with approval, Vance always found a way to dampen spirits and impede progress.

Danny wondered if there were a way to squeeze Vance out of the picture, but Christian ethics made it hard to seriously consider such a move. On the other hand, how could he take the business to the next level with Vance pulling on his coattails?

Tiggers and Eeyores never make a comfortable team. They need each other. They balance and complement each other, but resistance and misunderstandings are commonplace.

In this particular case, Danny-the-Tigger would do well to consider more than his own feelings of irritation. Vance-the-Eeyore might be a God-sent balance, keeping the business out of the ditch and putting food on the table for the next generation of Bishops.

Eeyore and Owl

A conversation between Eeyore and Owl can make an observer feel as if he has walked into a double-feature movie with both films running concurrently—and on the same screen.

"I sure hope Pastor Ryan doesn't preach on Jeremiah again this Sunday," said Charlene as she adjusted her skirt and slipped into a new pair of heels. "I can't get much out of the Old Testament."

"Did you say Jeremiah?" her husband asked. "Always loved that book. Lots of good quotes in Jeremiah."

"Sermons written in a series seem so artificial," she replied. "Everything is planned in advance. Just doesn't seem right."

"Plans?" Philip fished in the closet for his new shirt. "Yes, there's a good quote about plans. Jeremiah 29:11 says God knows the plans he has for us."

"If we don't make room for spontaneity, people will become bored." Charlene pursed her lips as she applied Pink Illusion with a brush.

"The crowds have been a little light the past few weeks. I am not sure we need more room," her husband noted as he patted his pockets and tried to remember where he'd put his change and keys.

It is only natural that Owl and Eeyore talk *at* each other rather than *to* one another. They have completely different thinking processes. That is precisely why they have less friction between them. It is difficult to be offended when you haven't listened to a word the other person has said!

This lack of attention is not rooted in animosity or indifference. Owl and Eeyore have a lot in common. They both are problem centered. Owl enjoys problems because they are a mental challenge. Looking at situations from a hundred different angles is second nature to him. Eeyore enjoys problems because they confirm his already negative outlook on life and provide hours of fodder for rumination.

All in all, Charlene-the-Eeyore and Philip-the-Owl will make boon companions. But don't expect either of them to actually solve anything. That doesn't appear to be the purpose for which God made them.

The Lord God Made Them All

In the mid-1800s Cecil Alexander looked around at the world of infinite variety and wrote: "All things bright and beautiful, / All creatures great and small, / All things wise and wonderful, / The Lord God made them all."[6]

Ah, what wisdom in this childhood rhyme! If we could only remember that the Lord God made us all and that he delights in the varied cornucopia formed by his hands, our attitudes toward each other would mellow a great deal. Yet we forget that simple truth so quickly. This is surprising because the concept really has been around since the beginning.

Long before Alexander picked up his pen, the writer of Psalms said, "Know that the LORD, He is God; it is He who has made us, and not we ourselves; we are His people and the sheep of His pasture" (Psalm 100:3).

God made us. Not impersonal forces of an evolving universe. Not big bangs or primordial slime charged with a lightning strike. Not accidental happenstances and billions upon billions of years toiling up the evolutionary ladder.

God *made* us. All of us were his idea. Different nations. Different skin tones. Different desires, dreams, music styles, senses of humor, clothing preferences, jobs, and environments. Desert dwellers. Mountain people. City slickers. Village keepers. When the psalmist wrote the above quote, millions of people populated the earth. Looking at all of them, he said that God *made*.

God made *us*. Not that the Almighty started out with a good plan but is now stumbling along with a creation gone wild. Not that he is surprised we turned out so rotten, twisted, or such a far cry from the single, perfect copy he desired. Imperfection, personality clashes, sour people with hidden agendas, and more are not surprises to God. He knew what was ahead when he breathed life into Adam's clay. All people are not good, but all people are his property.

Sin is real, and humans are all in need of redemption. God is a holy judge who will one day send fire on all that offends. Earth and the people on it have been scarred and spiraling downward since Eden. But that gloomy reality has nothing to do with the infinite variety of personalities God has created. It is not wrong for Eeyore to be Eeyore. Neither is it inherently wrong for someone to be phlegmatic, golden retriever, red, ITNJ . . . or even XYZ! Personality differences, including ones that clash with our own styles, are not sin. God delights in differences, and we can learn from them.

If we truly believe the Lord God made us all, we have to agree that only *he* has the right to judge us all. Accepting that fact at the heart level should spare us a bundle of useless frustration. We should take each situation at face value and respond to the behaviors rather than get bent out of shape trying to make others think, feel, or see how things "ought" to be. People don't have to be like us—and we don't have to be like them—before we can accept each other.

If we truly believe the Lord God made us all, we will value the advice, correction, and ideas of others without being threatened by them. We also can go against their advice without guilt or fear. Because the Lord made us all, all stand on level ground. Each can have his own ideas. Each makes valuable contributions. Each is worth listening to. And in the end, each must be responsible for the conduct of his own life.

If we truly believe the Lord God made us all, and we acknowledge that God makes no mistakes, then we will realize he has created nothing without purpose. So surely, we are all needed, and we all need each other just as he created us. Romans 8:28 assures us that "all things work together for good to those who love God." That principle is true now . . . and forever. That principle is true in relationships—and yes, even when you live with an Eeyore.

After all, Eeyore must live with you too.

> GET THE POINT

God has placed an infinite variety of personalities within his creation for a reason.

> > READ THE BOOK

Look up 1 Thessalonians 5:14.

1. In this passage Paul exhorts the Christians to react four different ways in response to four different types of people. What are the types, and how should we respond to each?

2. Can you think of specific people in your life who are similar in temperament to Rabbit, Piglet, Tigger, and Owl? Which are you?

Study Isaiah 28:23-29.

1. Although these verses discuss various types of grain, verse 29 lets us know that more is being discussed here than farming. This portion of Isaiah is about God's judgment. How would you make application of this Scripture?

2. Do you see a similarity between the modern saying "Different strokes for different folks" and this passage? Why or why not?

Read Romans 14:1-13.

1. The Christians in Rome came from various backgrounds and were at different levels of spiritual maturity. How did Paul say believers were to respond to the great variety of opinions and customs found among them?

2. What would be a modern-day parallel of the situation faced in the Roman church?

>>> TELL THE TRUTH

1. Have you ever been labeled as a certain personality type? Recall that occasion. Were you surprised to be assigned that personality type?

2. Is it beneficial to group personalities according to types? Why or why not?

3. What are three specific ways that your personality and that of Eeyore work for mutual benefit?

>>>> REVIEW THE POINTS

1. There is a use for everything in God's economy, even difficult people.

2. Even though someone may irritate you, he or she is not necessarily sick, weird, or flawed.

3. When a problem person enters your life, looking for the good can make the trial less severe.

4. Being a good listener to a critical Eeyore is not easy, but with wisdom it can be done.

5. It takes thought, heart, and practice to communicate effectively.

6. Christians have a responsibility to spur one another on to good deeds and better character development, and sometimes that involves a loving confrontation.

7. God has placed an infinite variety of personalities within his creation for a reason.

NOTES

1. The American Medico-Psychological Association (which later became the American Psychiatric Association or APA) first tried to classify "sick" emotions in 1918. After nine published tries, they came out with the first *DSM* in 1952. This was said to be the final word on who was sick and who was well. But the final word kept changing. The *DSM II* arrived in 1968. It was followed by the *DSM III* (1980), the *DSM III-R* (1987), and the *DSM IV* (1994). Between *DSM III-R* and *DSM IV*, nearly a hundred new ways to be mentally ill were added to the book, and the number keeps growing. *DSM V* may be published before this book is off the press.

2. Criteria has been simplified and shortened for lay readership.

3. Alfred Lord Tennyson. www.brainyquote.com.

4. A simple professional source in which to read more about Hippocrates' view is: "Hippocrates of Cos" by Ludwig Edelstein, in *The Encyclopedia of Philosophy*, vol. 4, editor in chief Paul Edwards (New York: Macmillan Publishing Company / London: Collier Macmillan Publishers, 1967), 6.

5. One book that outlines the personalities by color is *The Color Code: A New Way to See Yourself, Your Relationships, and Life* by Taylor Hartman (New York: Scribner Book Company, 1999).

6. Cecil Alexander, *Hymns for Little Children* (1848), www.firstscience.com.